The Rich Hermana

A FIRST-GEN GUIDE TO MONEY, MINDSET, AND WEALTH

(No Matter Where You Started)

IXAMAR PALUMBO

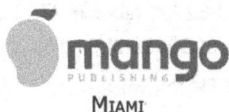

mango
PUBLISHING

MIAMI

Copyright © 2025 by Ixamar Palumbo.
Published by Mango Publishing, a division of Mango Publishing Group, Inc.

Cover Design: Elina Diaz
Cover Photo/Illustration: Elina Diaz
Interior Illustrations: stock.adobe.com/Marina Zlochin
Layout & Design: Elina Diaz

For permission requests, please contact the publisher at:
Mango Publishing Group
5966 South Dixie Highway, Suite 300
Miami, FL 33143
info@mango.bz

For special orders, quantity sales, course adoptions and corporate sales, please email the publisher at sales@mango.bz. For trade and wholesale sales, please contact Ingram Publisher Services at customer.service@ingramcontent.com or +1.800.509.4887.

The Rich Hermana: A First-Gen Guide to Money, Mindset, and Wealth (No Matter Where You Started)

Library of Congress Cataloging-in-Publication number: 2025938534
ISBN: (print) 978-1-68481-829-7, (ebook) 978-1-68481-830-3
BISAC category code: BUS050030 BUSINESS & ECONOMICS / Personal Finance / Money Management

For my daughter, Mila. *Mi hija.*

This book is my love letter and legacy to you: a piece of generational wealth filled with the guidance I wish I had when I was younger.

May it remind you that your voice, your dreams, and your freedom are worth protecting and passing down.

"La vida es para ser feliz."

—Abuelita

TABLE OF CONTENTS

INTRODUCTION

MY FIRST MONEY MEMORY

"Nadie te quita lo que está pa' ti."

Let's play a game. I'll tell you about my first money memory as a kid of immigrant parents, and you can take a wild guess as to why my relationship with money has been a hot mess ever since. Ready?

Okay, I'm kidding…kind of. We'll come back to it.

First, let's get one thing straight: I'm not a licensed financial guru or a money wizard. I don't have all the answers on how to get rich, stay rich, or turn your budget into a masterpiece. That's not my lane. But what I do have is the real, lived experience of figuring out money on my own as a first-gen Latina raised to believe that hard work alone is the key to success.

And here's the thing: personal finance is *personal*, but the conversations around it shouldn't be reserved for just financial professionals. Yes, some topics like tax law, investment strategies, and estate planning are best explained by experts. You won't find deep dives on those here. But spending money—on things like nutrition, fitness, or even learning about fashion—is something we all navigate in our own way. And that's exactly why these conversations need to happen among *real* people, sharing what's worked, what hasn't, and what we're still figuring out along the way.

If you're reading this, chances are you know exactly what that means.

Being first-gen in the United States, whether you were born here or immigrated young, means a lot more than just being the first in your family to go to college or land a corporate job. It means figuring out money on your own while carrying the weight of your family's sacrifices.

I've been there. I was the kid translating bank statements at the kitchen table, the college student drowning in financial aid paperwork, and the adult trying to balance saving, investing, and helping family do the same. I know what it's like to navigate the American financial system that wasn't built with us in mind, and I've spent years learning how to make it work for us anyway.

That's why I wrote this book: not as a financial expert, but as a first-gen daughter who watched her mom survive, figure things out, and grow right alongside me. I'm not here to preach, just to keep it real and hold us accountable.

Because I am The Rich Hermana, the rich big sis you needed growing up. And big sis doesn't sugarcoat things. So buckle up, because we're diving deep into everything, including money and mindset, and yeah, we might even unpack a little generational trauma while we're at it.

Being first-gen and the child of immigrant parents comes with a whole lot of pressure. Explaining that weight to your nonimmigrant friends? Whew. It's mental gymnastics. It usually goes something like this when I try to explain it to the Marys and Steves of my world:

"It's like you're carrying this invisible backpack, filled with all your parents' dreams...the ones they couldn't chase because they were too busy building a better life for you."

"You want to build a career, make good money, and live comfortably, but the weight of their sacrifices is always there, pushing down on you."

"It's like walking a tightrope where you're trying to balance your dreams while honoring everything your parents gave up. I want to buy a house for myself, but I should buy one for my mom first."

Sound familiar?

Here's the good part: by the end of this book, you'll understand precisely why you feel the way you do about money and how we can change that together. We'll first connect the dots between your upbringing, your family's struggles, and the money habits you've picked up. Once you see the patterns, you can spot and ditch the limiting beliefs that have been holding you back.

We're not just understanding the "why." We're building a healthier, more you-friendly relationship with money, the kind we should've learned about way earlier in life. And since this book isn't just for reading but for *doing*, you'll find activities and reflections throughout. So, if this book resonates with you, do me a favor: pass it on to another *hermana* or *hermano* who could benefit from learning the basics of financial literacy sooner than you did.

Just maybe *don't* write in it if you plan to pass it down...unless you want them to see all your money *aha* moments firsthand. In that case, highlight away.

Remember those mental gymnastics? We're aiming for the first-gen money Olympics. Class is in session.

We're done with the constant stress and anxiety around money. We're boosting your confidence to make financial decisions, big or small, and flipping the script from scarcity to abundance. No more playing small. We're going after the financial goals that actually matter to you.

Here's how it's going down.

First, we'll tackle the unique financial challenges of being first-gen kids of immigrants, whether you were born in your parents' new country or immigrated with them, like figuring out systems that weren't taught to us by our parents.

Remember translating government documents for family when you were ten? Yep, we'll touch on how those experiences shaped your financial habits, but more importantly, we'll find your "why" first: the reason managing your money will finally feel personal, not just practical. Don't worry; this isn't about sitting in the past. We're not here to marinate in old money wounds. We're here to celebrate how far you've come, flip the script on scarcity, and build an abundance mindset that sticks while getting into the "how" of it all.

Here's what you can also expect:

❖ **Budgeting 101:** Not the bland, restrictive kind. We're talking realistic, flexible budgeting that works with your paycheck and lifestyle.

❖ **Saving with a Purpose:** No more "just in case" funds gathering dust. By creating a clear path, we're saving for generational wealth, dream goals, and the life you want.

❖ **Investing Basics:** You don't need to be rich to invest. I'll show you how to start small, stay consistent, and grow your money without feeling overwhelmed.

❖ **Credit Building:** From your first credit card to decoding your credit score, I'm explaining everything in simple, stress-free terms that make sense.

❖ **The Side Quests:** What's passive income? Here's how you can get your nine-to-five to finance that side hustle until it takes off.

When you finish this book, managing your money won't feel like a chore; it'll feel like you're finally in control. Honestly? You might even enjoy it. Throughout this book, I'll drop tools, tips, and resources to make this journey easier, including

budgeting apps, checklists, and names of organizations that
can help you navigate the system in the United States.

This book is your guide: a trusted resource you'll return to
whenever you need a reminder or a little extra push. So, grab
a pen, take notes, highlight your favorite parts, and apply
what you learn immediately. Your future self will thank you.

"Nadie te quita lo que está pa' ti."

What is meant for you will never be taken away, no matter the
obstacles or setbacks along the way.

It's about trusting in your own power, knowing that every
lesson learned, every risk taken, and every step forward is part
of a bigger picture. When doubt creeps in, let these words
remind you that no one can strip away your potential, your
dreams, or the knowledge you gain along the way.

Real generational wealth goes beyond money. We're passing
down wisdom, breaking cycles, and equipping the next
generation with tools we never had. We're creating a legacy
of financial confidence, resourcefulness, and ownership.
We're making informed choices, understanding how
money works, and ensuring that wealth, both financial and
intellectual, flows *through* our families, not just *to* them.

At the end of the day, I want you to feel empowered to chase
your dreams and honor your family in a way that feels deeply
true to you. Because let's be real, when we start pouring into
our own cup by educating ourselves, taking control, and

shifting our mindset, that's how we build generational wealth that lasts.

We'll get there, *hermana*. Now, let's get to work.

My First Money Memory

"Más vale pájaro en mano que cien volando."

My first money memory dates back to Y2K. It was the end of 1999, and we were in the middle of the Pokémon hype before winter break. I was nine. I couldn't afford Pokémon cards, so I'd usually bum one of the reject cards from a classmate, my version of Pokémon dumpster diving.

Then, my mother invested in the family office printer for Christmas.

To my nine-year-old self, that printer was pure magic. I learned every trick it had, even using the World Wide Web to print my favorite Pokémon characters. So, I masterminded a plan to fit in with the kids who *could* afford these trading cards.

I started by printing a bunch of Pokémon stencils, mainly the big names like Pikachu and Charizard. I'd draw my own versions using those stencils when the printer ink ran low. I'd bring my creations to class, color them in, and produce vibrant Pokémon collages that I stuck onto my composition notebooks. Before long, word spread: I was known as the go-to Pokémon artist.

"I'll give you this quarter if you give me a full-page Pikachu."
Thus, my first business venture was born.

But I didn't stop there. I soon discovered I could turn our
family's Olive Garden outings into another opportunity.
Every weekend, while my mom treated us to a fancy dinner,
I'd casually "borrow" a couple of boxes of crayons from the
restaurant's kid's menu stash. With those crayons, I began
selling what I dubbed "premium Pokémon coloring supplies"
for another quarter.

My Pokémon hustle quickly became legendary—proof that
even at nine, I was already mastering the fine art of business.

There's an old Spanish saying, *"Más vale pájaro en mano
que cien volando"*: a bird in the hand is worth more than a
hundred flying. Those reject cards, that magical printer, the
chain restaurant crayons. Even as a kid, I learned to value
what was right in front of me instead of chasing after what I
couldn't have. It's a reminder that sometimes, making the most
of what you possess is the most brilliant move.

Now that we're diving into the topic of your first money
memory, it's time for our first exercise to get these creative
juices flowing. I want you to reflect on your own experiences
with money. Reading about personal finance is just the
appetizer; exploring your history and finances is the Michelin
Star entrée. *Yum!*

CHAPTER 1

THE CORE OF PERSONAL FINANCE

*"Honra y dinero se ganan despacio
y se pierden ligero."*

I know, I know. You're like, "Where's the part where we talk *dinero*?!"

Before we dive into some money talk, we're taking a detour into *el propósito*. Stick with me.

Here's the thing: to truly rewire our financially un-savvy brains, we need to discover our life's purpose and connect it with our ideal financial journey. Trust me, it's less woo-woo than it sounds, but light a *velita* if you have to.

Think of this as the launch pad for your financial success, fast-tracking your wealth-building journey. This will be your foundation where we lay the groundwork for a transformative experience that empowers you to take charge of your finances with intention, without feeling overwhelmed or intimidated. We're honoring our past and embracing a brighter tomorrow, leaving behind any resentment toward those we thought would teach us about money.

It's in the past. We're focusing on the now, and these bills need to get *paid*.

Growing up as the child of immigrant parents, I was raised to believe that every achievement demanded relentless sacrifice: a perspective that echoes across so many immigrant households, from Latinx to Southeast Asian, African, Middle Eastern, Caribbean, and beyond. Yet, over time, I've come to realize there's another way: one where success doesn't have to be hard-won at the expense of every bit of your spirit. Instead of feeling compelled to battle every obstacle, I discovered that embracing opportunities with balance and grace can lead to a fulfilling life without the weight of constant sacrifice like the one our parents carried.

This outlook resonates with a Spanish saying I often recall: "*Honra y dinero se ganan despacio y se pierden ligero.*" In essence, honor and money are not trophies to be seized overnight but treasures cultivated through thoughtful effort, earned slowly, yet vulnerable to vanishing quickly if we aren't careful.

Ultimately, the goal is to move with intention and patience. Every deliberate, heart-led step not only enriches our character but also builds a stable foundation for lasting financial and personal success.

So, have grace with yourself.

In the quiet moments before the chaos of the day unfolds, take a gentle pause to honor where you are on your journey. Ask yourself, *What is it that ignites my spirit every morning?* Is it the yearning to break free from the chains of financial insecurity, or the dream of a life bursting with joy, abundance, and purpose?

For me, my "why" is woven into the very fabric of my identity. I live to honor the legacy of my immigrant mother, who fought tirelessly for her rightful place in this world. And while my story is rooted in the Latinx experience, I know I'm not alone. Whether your family came from the Dominican Republic, Nigeria, Vietnam, Lebanon, Haiti, or El Salvador, so many of us share this thread of sacrifice, hustle, and hope. Our stories may vary in language and tradition, but the resilience? That's universal. Each day, I strive to honor my mother's struggles by embodying the role of the big sister I wish I'd had, guiding you with the same warmth and unwavering support. Her courage reminds me that while our paths may be steeped in hardship, they can also be paved with gentle strength and compassion.

Understanding what drives you is not just a nice-to-have; it's the cornerstone of building a life and a financial future that resonates deeply with who you are. Think about it like building healthier habits with food. When you understand *why* you want to feel stronger or have more energy, making nourishing choices becomes second nature, not just a temporary task. The same applies to your financial journey. When you connect with your core motivations, every step you take becomes infused with purpose and value, transforming challenges into opportunities for growth.

So, let's break this down together, like two besties in deep conversation. Time to explore the heart of your aspirations, uncovering the dreams and desires that make you unique. Remember: this thoughtful, intimate journey is about celebrating your resilience, cherishing your progress, and moving forward with intention and grace.

The Purpose Path Exercise: Reflect, Identify, Visualize

Reflect: Get Comfy and Dig Deep

Before you make better money moves, you have to have your head on straight. *La cabeza bien puesta.* You need to have your thinking cap on and to be laser-focused on your goals. It all ties together to create systems in place that will eventually be automated in your brain. Positive financial decisions and boundaries will become second nature to you.

You have to tackle the mind before you tackle your wallet.

Just like your physical goals, the lifestyle change can't be temporary. Consistency is key, and practice does make perfect.

This chapter is your invitation to explore the journey of who you are: where you've been, what lights you up today, and where you're headed tomorrow. You're granting yourself a heartfelt conversation with your inner child, steeped in the resilience and warmth of our families' sacrifices, whether they came here with a suitcase full of hope, a head full of dreams, or both.

Begin by finding your happy place. Maybe it's that sunlit corner in your home where memories of *abuela*'s kitchen linger, your favorite local coffee shop where each sip of *café con leche* feels like a warm hug, or a quiet park bench that reminds you of peaceful afternoons spent with family. This is your sanctuary: a space where you can be completely, unapologetically you.

Now, grab your journal or open your notes app, and take a journey back to *your earliest money memory*. It might be the thrill of earning your very first dollar by helping out at home, the bittersweet lesson from a first job where that paycheck vanished in bills, or the defining moment when a family crisis taught you the true weight of financial uncertainty. For each memory, jot down not only the details but also the emotions you felt (panic? hope? urgency?) and the lessons they carried. These feelings are clues to what truly drives you.

Maybe your family never talked about money out of fear, or maybe financial survival meant working cash jobs under the table. Whether you were raised in a Haitian, Korean, Indian, or Guatemalan household, those early money messages stick with us...and rewriting them starts here.

Keep in mind, research on narrative identity shows that the stories we tell ourselves, complete with the emotions they evoke, shape our self-concept and future choices. As one study put it:

*"People living in modern societies provide their
lives with unity and purpose by constructing
internalized and evolving narratives of the self."*[1]

Expressive writing isn't just a creative outlet; it's a proven
way to process emotions and foster personal growth. That
anxious moment when money was scarce may reveal your
deep need for security, while saving up for something special
might remind you of the beauty of patience. Look for recurring
themes: if many memories involve stepping up for your family,
perhaps support is your ultimate goal; if your heart leaps at the
thought of a passion project, creativity could be your true fuel.

By strengthening your mindset, you create a foundation for
financial success. The way you think about money, discipline,
and wealth-building will dictate your long-term progress.
Your thoughts shape your habits, and your habits shape your
results. It starts in your mind, but it manifests in your reality.

1. **What is your earliest money memory?**
   Describe the situation in detail. Who was involved,
   what happened, and how did it make you feel?

   _____

   _____

   _____

1 Dan P. McAdams, "The Psychology of Life Stories," *Review of General Psychology* 5, no. 2 (2001):
   100–122, https://doi.org/10.1037/1089-2680.5.2.100.

2. **What emotions come up when you think about money today?** Do you feel anxiety, confidence, excitement, fear? How do these emotions connect to your early experiences?

_____

_____

_____

3. **What lessons about money did you learn from your family or culture?** Were they empowering or limiting? How have they influenced your financial decisions so far?

_____

_____

_____

4. **If you could rewrite your money story, what would it look like?** What beliefs, habits, or patterns would you change to align with the financial future you want?

_____

_____

_____

5. **What is one financial value or goal that matters most to you right now?** Whether it's security, freedom, generosity, or legacy, I want you to define it and explore why it's important to you.

_____

_____

_____

Identify: What Lights You Up?

Now that you've revisited your past, let's shift our focus to today. Before we go any further, let's get one thing straight: building wealth isn't just about making more money. It's about making *aligned* money: the kind that doesn't require you to sell your soul or sacrifice your joy. And to get there, you need to cultivate a mindset that prioritizes both purpose and profit.

For many of us who grew up in immigrant households, the idea of choosing work based on joy, not just survival, can feel unfamiliar, even privileged. When you've seen your parents hustle out of necessity, it's hard to shake the belief that financial security means sacrificing passion...but breaking that cycle starts with us.

We're not forcing ourselves into a "dream job" mold based on what sounds good on paper. We're recognizing the activities that make us feel alive, even if they don't immediately come with a paycheck. Why? Because when you understand what truly lights you up, you can make financial decisions that align with your values rather than ones driven by scarcity or obligation. The right mindset keeps you from chasing money for money's sake and focuses on building wealth. It helps you create a life where money works for you, not the other way around.

Think about those little moments when time seems to disappear. Maybe you get lost in a book, feel at home in the kitchen experimenting with new recipes, or love planning the perfect gathering for friends and family. These aren't just hobbies; they're clues. They reveal what energizes you and what values shape your decisions. That includes decisions around money.

Psychologist Mihaly Csikszentmihalyi calls this state of deep involvement "flow." Csikszentmihalyi proposes that when we engage in activities that bring us this sense of focus and fulfillment, we don't just boost our creativity; we elevate our entire well-being. When you learn to cultivate this mindset, your financial habits naturally follow. You start setting goals based on what truly matters, rather than just chasing the next paycheck or following someone else's definition of success.

"Flow is the state in which people are so involved in an activity that nothing else seems to matter." [2]

Flow keeps you from feeling like you're running in circles, stuck in a cycle of working just to get by, without a clear path forward. Instead of feeling trapped in the rat race, flow expands your vision, helping you recognize opportunities that

---

2 Mihaly Csikszentmihalyi, *Flow: The Psychology of Optimal Experience* (Harper Perennial Modern Classics, 2008), 57. Kindle.

align with your true calling, ones that don't just bring in money but also create lasting fulfillment and effortless abundance.

Ask yourself:

❖   What activities make you lose track of time?
❖   What do you love doing, even if no one paid you for it?
❖   What brings a sense of purpose into your everyday life?

If cooking elaborate meals reminds you of the love and hospitality passed down from *mamá* or *abuela*, that's a sign that nurturing others is core to who you are. If you thrive when hosting gatherings, community might be your driving force. If your heart skips a beat when you create, then self-expression is essential to your happiness.

Not sure what excites you yet? Experiment. Here's how you can experiment with discovering your passion *for free or at a low cost*:

Try a Low-Stakes Side Hustle

Sell digital prints by creating a free Canva account and using royalty-free design resources. Sell them on Etsy, which has lower fees than selling physical products. If writing is your thing, offer freelance gigs on Fiverr or Upwork. Both allow you to list services for free while taking a commission once you land a gig. Do you like flipping thrift finds? Start by selling clothes you already own on Poshmark or Facebook Marketplace before investing in inventory.

Take a Class for Fun

Many places offer a "first class free" trial for dance, yoga, or fitness. Platforms like Coursera, Skillshare (free trial), and Udemy (discounted courses) offer affordable online learning. If you're into coding or marketing, Google and HubSpot provide free certification courses. Your local library may also host free workshops or offer access to learning platforms.

Volunteer in a Field That Interests You

Join VolunteerMatch.org or check local Facebook groups for opportunities to help at events, community projects, or shelters. If you're curious about social media management, offer to help a nonprofit with their Instagram or TikTok presence for free to build experience.

Start a Passion Project

Launch a blog for free on WordPress, Substack, or Medium, or start a YouTube or TikTok channel with just your phone. If you're into podcasting, record using free apps like Spotify for Creators and use Canva for free cover art. If you love photography, start with your phone and edit using free apps like Lightroom Mobile.

Teach Something You Enjoy

Charge $5 per class and teach at a free community space like a park. Use platforms like Eventbrite (free for free events) or Facebook Events to spread the word. Eventually, you can land sponsors to offer free classes while getting paid. If you prefer online teaching, use Google Meet or Zoom's free plan or create a TikTok/Instagram page sharing bite-sized lessons.

Shadow Someone in a Career That Interests You

Reach out to people on LinkedIn and ask if you can shadow them for a day or interview them about their work; many professionals are open to sharing insights if you ask respectfully. Attend virtual career panels and free webinars to hear from industry experts.

Attend Networking or Industry Events

Many local meetups, chamber of commerce events, and university alumni gatherings are free to attend. Websites like Meetup.com, Eventbrite, and LinkedIn Events list free networking opportunities. If you're into tech or business, try Google Startup events and free WeWork networking sessions.

Switch Up Your Environment

A fresh perspective doesn't require a plane ticket. Visit a local museum on a free admission day, explore a new neighborhood, or work from a public library for a change of scenery. If travel excites you, apply for travel scholarships or house-sitting gigs through platforms like TrustedHousesitters.

Revisit Childhood Hobbies

If you love drawing, grab free coloring pages or use digital drawing apps. If you are into music, borrow an instrument from your local library or find free online tutorials on YouTube. Writing? Start a free journal on Notion or Google Docs.

Do a "Thirty-Day Challenge"

Pick one free thing to try daily. Write one paragraph, learn five words in a new language (Duolingo), take a ten-minute online class, cook a new dish with pantry staples, or post a short video. Track what excites you most, then dive deeper.

But girl, with what time?!

The key is to start small and explore without pressure or guilt, especially if your time and energy are already stretched thin. If you're working multiple jobs or supporting family, this doesn't mean forcing yourself into a new hobby when you're exhausted. It means looking for small sparks of joy in your current routine and making space for yourself when possible, even in micro-moments.

Maybe alignment doesn't look like starting a business tomorrow; it looks like noticing what excites you at work, what skills come naturally, or what parts of your job you enjoy more than others. It looks like asking yourself, "How can I make my current situation work better for me?" instead of feeling stuck in survival mode.

In my eyes, building wealth is about crafting a life that feels rich on your own terms: without guilt, without unrealistic timelines, and without feeling like you have to choose between survival and joy. Sometimes, you're in a season where making money is the priority, and that's okay. Alignment doesn't mean quitting everything to chase a dream; it means making intentional choices within your reality that get you closer to a future where you have more options.

So, if you're in a place where you need to chase the paycheck first, that's valid. We're not about to ignore financial responsibilities. We're building toward a life where money works for us, not the other way around.

Even if that starts with just five minutes of curiosity a day.

Because when you give yourself permission to dream beyond survival, even in small ways, you slowly start shifting the cycle for yourself and for the generations that come after you.

Visualize: See It Before You Build It

Before we start mapping out financial goals, let's take a step back. Because here's the truth: you can't budget, save, or invest your way to true wealth if your mindset is still operating from a place of scarcity. If deep down, you believe money is just about survival, you'll always play defense: cutting costs, hustling harder, and feeling like there's never enough. Intentional wealth-building is about designing a life where financial freedom allows you to focus on what truly matters.

That's why we don't just dive into spreadsheets and vision boards right away.

First, we *align.*

We get clear on what kind of life we actually want, not just the one we've been conditioned to chase out of obligation. This doesn't mean abandoning financial responsibility overnight. It means creating space, however small, to define what financial freedom actually looks like for you beyond just "making ends meet."

For some, it's time freedom: the ability to work less and still be financially secure. For others, it's stability: not living paycheck to paycheck or worrying about emergency expenses. For many, it's having *options*: the ability to choose work that aligns with their values, to support loved ones without burnout, and to make decisions without fear.

If you're already stretched thin, your visualization needs to be simple, low-maintenance, and effective: something that helps you stay focused, not something that feels like just another task on your to-do list.

The "Five-Minute Future Self" Exercise

Instead of a complex vision board, you can take five minutes to answer the following:

- ❖ If I had more financial stability, what would my life look like in one year?
- ❖ What would change in my daily routine if I wasn't constantly worried about money?
- ❖ What would I finally have time or energy for?

Write it down in a note on your phone, a journal, or even voice-record it. No fancy setup needed, just clarity. The goal isn't a perfect roadmap; it's to start shifting your focus from survival to possibility.

Vision Board Lite: A Quick & Low-Effort Alternative

If you're more visual, create a "vision album" on your phone instead of a traditional vision board. Save five to ten images that represent your financial goals, whether that's a debt-free notification, a peaceful home, a family vacation, or a thriving business. Look at it weekly as a reminder that you're building something bigger than just your next paycheck.

The "One-Goal Focus" Method

Feeling overwhelmed by long-term planning? Start with one priority at a time. Instead of thinking *I need to save, invest, pay off debt, start a side hustle, and take care of my family*, simplify:

❖ **Short-term (next six months):** What's the one financial move that would give you the most breathing room? (Example: "Save one month's worth of expenses" or "Increase income by $300/month.")

❖ **Long-term (three to five years):** What's one thing you'd love to be financially possible? (Example: "Work one job instead of two," "Land a remote job," or "Own a home.")

By focusing on one move at a time, you prevent goal paralysis.

Life shifts, and so should your financial plan. Survival mode isn't forever, but small habits now can help build a bridge out of it. Instead of strict tracking, do a quick five-minute financial check-in once a month:

❖ Did I make any progress toward my goal?

❖ What's one small thing I can do next month to move forward? (Example: increasing an automated transfer by $5, researching side gig ideas, updating your resume, or asking for a raise.)

❖ Am I still aligned with what I actually want, or do I need to adjust my focus?

Wealth is a lifestyle, not just a goal. And right now, your goal is to start creating options, even if they feel small. The point isn't to ignore reality; it's to start shifting out of survival mode in ways that actually work for you.

This is your permission to define wealth in a way that makes sense for your life: on your timeline, at your pace.

CHAPTER 2

BIG SISTER MONEY ADVICE

"No se ahogue en un vaso de agua."

Here's some big sister money advice I wish I'd known in my twenties! If any of these resonate, each concept is broken down in the next chapters. Let's get into it.

1. **Get comfortable with budgeting... It's not as scary as it sounds.** If budgeting feels like a punishment, let's flip that script. Budgeting isn't about restricting your spending; it's about giving yourself permission to spend intentionally. Think of it as mapping out your money so you can say "yes" to what matters most (hello, weekend getaways!) without guilt. We'll talk about easy, nonintimidating ways to start a budget that actually works for you. *Go to Chapter 3 for more on real-life budgeting!*

2. **While we're at it, let's create our Emergency Fund and our Sinking Funds.** This financial dynamic duo is your safety net. Your emergency fund saves the day when unexpected expenses strike (car

breakdowns, job loss, medical bills), while your sinking funds help you plan and save for specific goals, like vacations, holidays, or property taxes. These two will ideally live inside a high-yield savings account (HYSA) for maximum return thanks to our bestie, compound interest. *Go to Chapter 4 for more on savings with a purpose!*

3. **Dump your traditional savings account. HYSA is *that* girl.** The ultimate financial sidekick, a high-yield savings account, serves up high interest rates, flexibility, and FDIC insurance (Federal Deposit Insurance Corporation), so you can grow your savings, crush financial goals, and live your best financial life safely. In today's economy, we're aiming to stress less about inflation and enjoy easy access to our cash for when life starts life-ing and throws those unexpected curveballs. *Go to Chapter 5 for more on HYSAs!*

4. **Speaking of compound interest, have you checked up on your retirement accounts?** Listen, that night cream won't do much if you're stressing about money by the time you're ready to retire. The sooner you familiarize yourself with how easy it is to manage your retirement accounts, whether it's a basic 401k through your job or a Roth IRA (Individual Retirement Account) you open on your own, the sooner you'll be lying out on a hammock, stress-free, at sixty-five. Well...maybe not that soon, but you get my point. *Go to Chapter 10 for more on retirement accounts!*

5. **Your credit score is your financial reputation. Protect it.** Building a good credit score means you'll pay less in interest, have better access to loans, and enjoy financial perks that people without a strong score

just don't get. Think of it as that "A+" you're earning in Financial Adulthood 101. Start by paying bills on time, keeping balances low, and avoiding unnecessary debt. Your future self will thank you when you're getting better rates on things like car loans, mortgages, and even some jobs! *Go to Chapter 11 for more on building and protecting your credit!*

These are just the first steps to the foundation of financial independence. Building wealth, especially for women, means creating a world where you have options and choices.

No se ahogue en un vaso de agua.

Don't drown in a glass of water. You don't have to tackle it all at once; the best time to start was yesterday, but the second-best time is today. Baby steps are still steps. Let's keep building that financial confidence, one smart decision at a time.

CHAPTER 3

THE BUDGETING 101 BREAKDOWN

"Guarda el orden que el orden te guardará a ti."

Habits will make or break you. Sure, most people think budgets are restrictive. I get it. It used to feel that way for me, too. But a budget is actually a tool for freedom.

Guarda el orden que el orden te guardará a ti.

When you create structure in your finances, that structure will take care of you in return. It's like buying yourself time when you're questioning why there aren't enough hours in the day.

Instead of scrambling from paycheck to paycheck or wondering where your money went, a budget lets you decide in advance where you want it to go. You can splurge without guilt and save without sacrifice when in control. This chapter is about breaking down your budget in a way that feels right for you, not just following a formula.

Step 1: The Income Audit

Let's start with the foundation: your income. But here's the thing—we're not looking at your salary on paper, we're looking at what actually hits your bank account. That's your *net income*, a.k.a. the money you can actually spend.

A lot of people think they make $60K a year, but after taxes, insurance, and deductions, what they really see in their bank account is closer to $45K. That's the number that matters for your budget.

Let's make this easy. Open up your banking app and do the following:

❖ Go to your transaction history and filter by "Deposits" or "Incoming Transfers."

❖ Download your bank statements from the last twelve months (or scroll manually, if needed).

❖ If you have multiple income sources, categorize them: salary, freelance, side gig, etc.

❖ Write down your net income for each month to spot any patterns or inconsistencies.

Think of your income like a bucket of water. If the amount of water coming in changes every month, but your spending stays the same, you could run out before your next refill. A budget helps you see exactly how much water you have so you don't end up unexpectedly dry by week three.

Once you have your income numbers, you can:

❖ Take an average of the last twelve months (great if your income is stable).

OR

❖ Use your lowest-income month (ideal if your income fluctuates and you want extra financial wiggle room).

Meet Marisol

She works full-time as a social media manager ($3,800/month) but also sells custom crochet tops on the side. Some months her side gig brings in an extra $600; other months, it's just $200.

Here's what her income looks like:

❖ Lowest month: $3,800 (no extra sales)

❖ Highest month: $4,400 (hot girl summer demands crochet tops)

❖ Average: $4,000

If Marisol builds her budget based on her highest-income months, she might overspend and struggle when business is slow. Instead, she chooses to budget based on her lowest month, $3,800, so she's always prepared. Any extra income? That becomes bonus money for saving, investing into her business, investing for retirement, or guilt-free spending.

Step 2: Categorizing Expenses with the Traffic Light System

If you've never created a budget before, tracking your spending is the most eye-opening step. And yes, I mean tracking every single expense...even that late-night DoorDash order you forgot about.

For one month, log everything you spend. Use your:

- ❖ Bank statements
- ❖ Credit card transactions
- ❖ Receipts

At first, you might be shocked at where your money is actually going. But don't panic—this step is about awareness, not judgment. The goal is to see where your money naturally flows so we can build a budget that actually fits your life.

Now, instead of using generic spending categories, we're going to break your expenses into three easy-to-remember zones:

Red Zone:
Crucial, Fixed Expenses

These are the nonnegotiables: the bills that show up *every month, no matter what.*

This includes:

- ❖ Rent/mortgage
- ❖ Utilities (electricity, water, internet)
- ❖ Health insurance
- ❖ Minimum debt payments

A Rich Hermana Tip

If you're helping out family financially, include that here too! Some first-gen children of immigrants have *remesas* (money sent home) or monthly support for their parents. Treat it like a fixed expense so it's accounted for.

Yellow Zone: Crucial, Variable Expenses

These are necessary, but they fluctuate. You have some control over these costs, but they still need to be prioritized.

This includes:

- ❖ Groceries
- ❖ Gas/public transportation
- ❖ Household essentials (cleaning supplies, toiletries)

> **A Rich Hermana Tip**
>
> If your grocery bill is all over the place, take the average of the last three months to set a baseline.

Green Zone: Play Money (a.k.a. Joy Spending)

This is where your fun money lives: the spending that makes life feel good. We're not cutting everything, but budgeting for joy intentionally so you're not stressed later.

This includes:

- ❖ Eating out & coffee runs
- ❖ Shopping & hobbies
- ❖ Subscriptions (Netflix, Spotify, Audible)
- ❖ Self-care (nails, skincare, gym, hair appointments)

> **A Rich Hermana Tip**
>
> Instead of feeling guilty for spending in this category, think of it like, "I'm choosing how much joy I want to budget for."

Let's bring this to life with our friend Marisol, the social media manager and crochet queen. Here's how her monthly budget shakes out:

Red Zone (Fixed, Nonnegotiables)

- ❖ Rent: **$1,500**
- ❖ Utilities: **$150**
- ❖ Health insurance: **$200**
- ❖ Minimum credit card payment: **$100**
- ❖ Money sent to parents: **$300**

Yellow Zone (Variable, Necessary Expenses)

- ❖ Groceries: **$350**
- ❖ Gas & Ubers: **$120**
- ❖ Household essentials: **$50**

Green Zone (Play Money)

- ❖ Gym membership: **$50**
- ❖ Coffee & eating out: **$150**
- ❖ Subscriptions: **$30**
- ❖ Shopping & hobbies: **$75**

Total Monthly Spending: ~$3,075

Breaking your expenses into zones makes it clear where your money is going without getting stuck in overcomplicated budget categories.

❖ Red = The essentials that keep your life running

❖ Yellow = Flexible needs that you can tweak if needed

❖ Green = The fun stuff you budget for on purpose

This system helps you balance priorities without guilt, so you can pay your bills, enjoy life, and build wealth—all at the same time.

Step 3: Calculating Averages for Each Category

Now that you've sorted your expenses into the Red, Yellow, and Green Zones, it's time to crunch some numbers. This step is about seeing your true spending habits so you can build a budget that actually works for you.

Yes, it might feel a little tedious (*I see you avoiding your bank app*), but doing a full twelve-month snapshot gives you the most accurate picture of where your money really goes.

Think of this step like meal prepping. You wouldn't just guess how much food you need for the week. You check your fridge, take inventory, and plan accordingly.

Your bank statements = your financial fridge.

By looking at the past six to twelve months of spending, you're taking inventory of your finances so you can plan with confidence instead of guesswork.

How to Calculate Your Averages

1. **Pull Up Your Bank and Credit Card Statements**

   ❖ Go back at least *six months* (twelve months is even better!).

   ❖ Export your transactions or just scroll through manually.

2. **Group Expenses by Category**

   ❖ Using the *Red, Yellow, and Green Zones*, list your expenses for each month.

   ❖ You can do this in a spreadsheet, budgeting app, or even on paper.

3. **Calculate the Average for Each Category**

   ❖ Add up your spending for each category over the past months.

   ❖ Divide by the number of months to get your average.

Let's check back in with Marisol. After reviewing her bank statements, here's how her spending looks over three months:

Category	January	February	March	Average
Groceries	$325	$275	$459	**$353**
Transportation	$150	$160	$145	**$152**
Dining Out	$120	$200	$180	**$167**
Entertainment	$85	$90	$120	**$98**

What This Tells Marisol

❖ She thought she spent $300 on groceries, but her real average is $353, so she needs to budget accordingly.

❖ Some months she spends way more on dining out ($200 in February?!), so she might want to set a limit or up her income.

❖ Transportation stays pretty stable at $150-ish, so she can confidently budget for that amount.

Why This Step Works

❖ **No Guessing:** You now have real numbers to build a budget that reflects your actual spending.

❖ **Trend Spotting:** See where your money fluctuates so you can adjust accordingly.

❖ **No Surprises:** Knowing your true spending means fewer "uh-oh" moments before payday.

This is the blueprint for your budget, so take your time. Once you have your numbers, we'll move on to the next step: adjusting and optimizing your budget to fit your goals.

Step 4: Setting Spending Goals and Embracing Flexibility

Now that you have a clear picture, decide on target amounts for each zone. Keep flexibility in mind: if you love getting your nails done or trying new restaurants, budget for it in the Green Zone so you're not cutting out what brings you joy. We're creating a plan, not a prison. Some budgeting apps, like Monarch Money, already do this for you in case you're not into making spreadsheets or simply don't have the time.

Now let's tweak and adjust without stress. You might find that your spending is higher than your income in certain areas. Here's what to do:

1. **Start with the Green Zone**

See if there's any low-hanging fruit to trim here. Perhaps it's cutting that subscription you rarely use or reducing takeout meals. Small adjustments add up, and this zone is the easiest place to start.

2. **If Necessary, Move to the Yellow Zone**

If you find that tweaks in the Green Zone aren't enough, look for modest reductions here. Embrace the *"Hay comida en la casa"* movement and meal prep to lower grocery costs or carpool with a friend to trim transportation expenses. These changes can free up funds while keeping necessities in check.

3. **Last Resort: Red Zone Adjustments**

If you're still coming up short, explore options like negotiating a better rate on insurance, phone bills, subscriptions, or downsizing housing. These are big moves, so consider them carefully.

Step 5: The 50-30-20 Rule—A Blueprint for Balance

Now that you've mapped out your Red, Yellow, and Green Zones, it's time to decide how much of your income should go where. This rule helps ensure you're:

* ❖ **Covering necessities** (without stress)
* ❖ **Enjoying life** (without guilt)

- ❖ **Building wealth and financial security**
  (without feeling deprived)

Think of it like meal prepping for your money. You're allocating portions to what fuels your life today, while still making room for future goals.

The Breakdown

50% for Needs (Red & Yellow Zones)

Half of your income should go here. These cover the nonnegotiable expenses that keep your life running:

- ❖ Rent/mortgage
- ❖ Utilities (electricity, water, Wi-Fi)
- ❖ Groceries
- ❖ Transportation (gas, public transit)
- ❖ Insurance & minimum debt payments

A Rich Hermana Tip

Why do minimum debt payments belong in the Needs category? Making at least the *minimum payments* on your debt is *crucial* to maintaining a good credit score and avoiding costly penalties. Missing payments can lead to:

- ❖ Late fees
- ❖ Increased interest rates

> ❖ Credit score damage (making it harder to get loans or better financial opportunities)
>
> That's why minimum debt payments are classified under Needs. They keep you in good financial standing and prevent setbacks.

30% for Wants (Green Zone)

As discussed, this is your fun money for the things that make life enjoyable like:

- ❖ Eating out & coffee runs
- ❖ Streaming services & subscriptions
- ❖ Shopping & hobbies
- ❖ Travel & entertainment

> **A Rich Hermana Tip**
>
> Instead of feeling guilty for spending in this category, *budget for joy on purpose*. This way, you're enjoying life without wrecking your finances.

20% for Savings & Financial Goals

This chunk goes toward wealth-building activities like:

❖ Emergency fund (start by aiming for three to six months of expenses in savings)

❖ Extra debt payments (beyond the minimums)

❖ Retirement & investments

❖ Other financial goals (homeownership, starting a business, etc.)

A Rich Hermana Tip

Focus on your emergency fund first, then debt payoff.

Before throwing extra money at your debt, make sure you have at least a small emergency fund (around $1,000–$2,000) to cover unexpected expenses.

This way, if something happens, like losing your job or your car breaking down, you're not forced to rely on credit cards or loans to survive. Once you've saved at least one month of essential expenses, you can start balancing debt repayment and savings.

If your debt has super high interest (like credit cards with a 20% Annual Percentage Rate), you can shift more toward debt payoff after you have a financial safety net.

How Marisol Balances Saving & Debt Payoff

Since Marisol still has $5,000 in credit card debt (at a 22% interest rate), she needs a game plan. Instead of throwing all her extra cash at the debt immediately, she:

- ❖ Saves $1,500 in her emergency fund first (so she's not caught off guard).

- ❖ Then, she splits her 20% savings:

    - ❖ $400 toward extra debt payments

    - ❖ $200 toward her emergency fund (until she reaches three months' expenses)

    - ❖ $200 into her retirement investments

This way, she's paying down debt while still securing her future, instead of leaving herself financially vulnerable.

Marisol's Budget Breakdown Using the 50–30–20 Rule

Category	50–30–20 Rule	Marisol's Budget
Needs (50%)	$2,000	**$2,300 (58%)**
Wants (30%)	$1,200	**$900 (22%)**
Savings (20%)	$800	**$800 (20%)**

Why Marisol's Budget Looks Different

- ❖ She lives in a high-cost-of-living area, so her rent eats up a bigger chunk of her budget.

- ❖ To make up for it, she trims her "wants" category down to 22%.

- ❖ She still prioritizes savings at 20% because she's building her emergency fund and investing for retirement.

Your budget won't always fit the rule perfectly, and that's okay! Adjust where needed while keeping the overall balance in mind.

How to Adapt the 50–30–20 Rule for Your Life

- ❖ If your Needs exceed 50% → Trim your Wants or temporarily lower your savings percentage while working to reduce fixed expenses.

- ❖ If you're aggressively paying off debt → Shift more funds into savings and debt repayment.

- ❖ If you live in a high-cost-of-living area → Your Needs might require closer to 60%, so you'll need to adjust other areas accordingly.

Why This System Works

- ❖ **It's flexible:** You're not stuck with rigid numbers. You can adjust based on your situation.

- ❖ **It keeps you balanced:** You're not over-saving or overspending. You're doing both intentionally.

❖ **It helps you build wealth while still living your life:** Because let's be real, a budget shouldn't feel like punishment.

By following this approach, you'll have a budget that actually works for your life, not one that feels like a financial straitjacket.

Step 6: Make It Personal and Track in a Way That Works for *You*

Your budgeting journey should fit your lifestyle, not feel like another full-time job. The key to long-term success isn't just about numbers; it's about building a system that's effective, sustainable, and aligned with how you naturally manage money.

Think of your budget like a gym routine. Some people love lifting weights, others prefer yoga, and some thrive in group fitness classes. The best system is the one that allows you to enjoy the process and stick with it.

No single method works for everyone. Try different options until you find what clicks. Here are some popular ways to track spending:

Spreadsheet or Journal (Manual Tracking)

❖ **Best for:** People who like hands-on control.

❖ **Why it works:** Writing things down manually forces you to be more intentional with spending.

❖ **Try it if:** You enjoy bullet journaling, planners, or a visual approach to tracking money.

A Rich Hermana Tip

When I first started budgeting, I used a Google Sheet to track everything manually. It took time, but I really got to see where my money was going. Once I got into a groove, I switched to an app for convenience.

Budgeting Apps (Automated Tracking)

❖ **Best for:** People who want an easy, hands-off approach.

❖ **Why it works:** Apps like Monarch Money automatically categorize transactions and track spending trends.

❖ **Try it if:** You don't want to manually input every expense but still want visibility.

❖ **Note:** It is likely these apps will have an annual fee, so keep this expense in mind.

Envelope System (Cash-Based Budgeting)

❖ **Best for:** People who struggle with overspending, especially when dealing with cash income.

❖ **Why it works:** When you allocate your cash into specific categories (like groceries, fun money, or savings), you create built-in spending limits. Once the cash is gone, it's gone.

❖ **Try it if:** You tend to spend cash quickly without realizing where it went or you receive cash as part of your main income or side hustle and want better control over it.

A Rich Hermana Tip

If you get paid in cash from a side hustle, tips, or freelance work, it's easy to lose track of spending since it's not sitting in your bank account where you can see it. When I was first starting out as a lifestyle photographer in my twenties, I'd get paid a few hundred dollars in cash after each session. At first, I wasn't tracking where that money went, and it would disappear fast.

So, I started giving every dollar a job. Some went to help my mom with groceries, some went straight into my savings account to speed up my loan repayment, and the rest covered my dog's grooming and the landscapers. By intentionally dividing up my cash, I wasn't just guessing where my money went; I was making conscious choices that supported my responsibilities and financial goals.

Set It & Forget It (Automated Budgeting)

❖ **Best for:** People who want their budget to run on autopilot.

❖ **Why it works:** You set up auto-transfers to savings, debt payments, and investments so you're prioritizing financial goals without needing to think about it.

❖ **Try it if:** You want to eliminate decision fatigue and build good financial habits effortlessly.

A Rich Hermana Tip

Set up your savings and investments to transfer automatically right after payday. That way, you're paying yourself first before the money disappears into expenses.

Set Regular Budget Check-Ins to Hold Yourself Accountable

Weekly Check-Ins (Ten to Fifteen Minutes)

❖ Quickly review your spending to see if you're staying on track.

❖ Adjust if needed: maybe you overspent on groceries, so you can scale back on eating out.

Monthly Reviews

❖ Reflect on your spending habits.

❖ Where did you do well?

❖ Where can you improve?

❖ Adjust category allocations if needed.

Quarterly Adjustments

- ❖ Life changes. Income increases, expenses shift, and priorities evolve.

- ❖ Every three months, reassess your budget to ensure it aligns with your current goals.

A Rich Hermana Tip

When I first started tracking my spending, I thought I had a solid budget, but after a few months, I realized I was under-budgeting for groceries while over-budgeting for things I didn't actually need, like multiple streaming subscriptions. I had autopay set up for services I barely used, but I kept running out of grocery money faster than expected.

Once I took the time to review my spending, I canceled two streaming services and reallocated that money toward my savings and groceries. It was a small shift, but it made a huge difference in the long term. In the end, I was stressing less over fluctuating food expenses and I was making real progress toward my financial goals.

Your budget isn't set in stone. Some months will be more expensive than others, and that's okay. The goal is to stay aware and make intentional choices. If an unexpected expense pops up, adjust accordingly instead of abandoning your budget altogether.

For example, if you have a month where travel expenses exceed your Green Zone budget, you might cut back on dining out to balance things out.

Instead of seeing a budget as a restriction, think of it as a way to create financial peace. Budgeting isn't about saying "no" to things; it's about saying "yes" to the life you truly want. By staying mindful of your finances, you're giving yourself the gift of security, confidence, and financial freedom.

No one gets budgeting perfect 100% of the time. If you overspend one month, don't stress. Adjust and move forward. The most important thing is consistency. Over time, these small habits add up and create long-term financial success.

Your budget should work for you, not against you. *A tu manera.*

CHAPTER 4

SAVINGS WITH A PURPOSE

"Soldado advertido no muere en guerra."

Imagine your car breaks down unexpectedly, leaving you stranded on the side of the road: no quick fix, no magic solution, just an unplanned expense that you're not financially ready to handle. For so many of us, that's what life without savings or a backup plan feels like.

A friend of mine once found herself in this exact situation. With no emergency fund to rely on and no family to help her, she had to put the car repairs on a high-interest credit card and delay paying other bills just to make ends meet. The stress was overwhelming. It felt like she was drowning in financial anxiety, constantly playing catch-up. But that moment became her wake-up call. She made a plan, started setting aside money little by little, and built her emergency fund over time. The peace of mind she gained was priceless. Knowing she had a safety net meant she could handle life's curveballs without panic, without the endless cycle of debt.

This was about security. It was about building a foundation that allowed her to focus on growing rather than just surviving.

Hermana, trust me. It's possible for you, too. Whether you're twenty-two or fifty-two, building an emergency fund can be a game-changer. Even if it feels like you're starting from zero, every dollar saved is a step toward a stronger, more resilient you.

So, What Is an Emergency Fund?

An emergency fund is exactly what it sounds like: money set aside for life's unexpected hits. This isn't for vacations, shopping sprees, or "almost emergencies" (you know, those moments when you convince yourself you *need* something right now). This also isn't a revolving fund where you're constantly transferring money back and forth into your checking account. The whole point here is to let that money sit and grow so that when a true emergency happens, you have a financial cushion ready to catch you.

Think of it as your financial seatbelt. You hope you never have to use it, but if an emergency happens, like losing your job, a surprise medical bill, or a car repair that just can't wait, you'll be glad it's there.

Soldado advertido no muere en guerra.

A warned soldier doesn't die in battle. This proverb my *abuelita* used to sing over and over is a powerful reminder that preparation is key to survival. When it comes to financial security, your emergency fund is your armor. Life's battles—the unexpected expenses, job losses, and medical emergencies— can come at any moment. Having money set aside means you are prepared, reducing the stress and devastation these financial blows can bring. Just like a soldier who enters battle with a plan and protection, you can face life's uncertainties with confidence when you have an emergency fund in place.

How Much Should You Save?

The general rule of thumb is to aim for three to six months' worth of living expenses. That might sound overwhelming, so let's break it down into manageable steps. Say hello to:

Your Emergency Fund Starter Checklist

Step 1: Know Your Baseline

- ❑ List your essential monthly expenses (rent, groceries, transportation, minimum debt payments)
- ❑ Multiply that total number by three → this is your first big goal
- ❑ Multiply by six → this is your stretch goal

Step 2: Set Your Microgoal

- ❏ Save your first $500
- ❏ Then your first $1,000
- ❏ Celebrate the small wins—you're building a safety net!

Step 3: Make It Automatic

- ❏ Set up automatic transfers, even if it's just $10–$50 per paycheck
- ❏ Add a calendar reminder if you're freelance or your income is irregular
- ❏ Try a "round-up" savings app that stashes spare change from your purchases

Step 4: Park It Where It Grows

- ❏ Open a HYSA
- ❏ Look for interest rates of 3%+
- ❏ Make sure you can transfer money quickly when needed without fees or penalties

Where Should You Keep It?

Your emergency fund should be accessible...but not *too* accessible. A high-yield savings account (HYSA) is a great option. Unlike traditional savings accounts at major banks like Bank of America, Chase, or Wells Fargo, a HYSA offers significantly higher interest rates. That means your money grows while it sits there looking cute waiting for emergencies.

What Do You Mean "My Money Grows" in a Savings Account?!

Yup! Here's how it works: when you deposit money into a savings account, the bank uses that money to lend to others or invest in financial opportunities. In return, they pay you interest as a "thank you" for letting them use your funds. HYSAs, which are often offered by online banks, provide even better rates because they save on costs like maintaining physical branches.

When you deposit money into a HYSA, your money earns interest just for sitting there. Unlike traditional savings accounts that offer around 0.01%, HYSAs can offer 3% or more.

Let's compare:

- ❖ $1,000 in a regular savings account = you earn 10 cents/year
- ❖ $1,000 in a HYSA at 4% = you earn $40/year

It's not going to make you rich, but it's better than nothing. Plus, the added benefit? Your emergency fund is out of sight, out of mind, so you're less tempted to touch it for nonemergencies.

These accounts create a mental barrier between your emergency fund and your everyday spending, making it less tempting to dip into for nonessentials. Just ensure the account allows quick transfers so your money is accessible when you *actually* need it. We'll go deeper into smart banking strategies in Chapter 5!

So, What Is a Sinking Fund?

"El que tiene tienda que la atienda."

While your emergency fund is the star of the show, sinking funds are the backup dancers.

Porque el que tiene tienda que la atienda.

If you have financial goals, you need to actively manage them in order to succeed. Sinking funds are your way of preparing for predictable expenses so they don't blindside you. These funds act as buckets or "vaults" within your savings account. Just like your emergency fund, sinking funds are earmarked for specific expenses you know are coming, like holiday gifts, car maintenance, or even that vacation to Italy you've been wanting to take mom on.

Planning for these in advance means you won't have to dip into your emergency fund for things that aren't actual emergencies.

Sinking funds don't need to be separate bank accounts, but they should be easy to track. Most people keep them inside the same HYSA where they keep their emergency fund, where their money can grow with interest while they save. Some banks even allow you to create sub-accounts or nickname your savings goals, so you can clearly label them as "Car Repairs" or "Travel Fund" instead of lumping everything together. If your bank doesn't have this feature, you can track your sinking funds on your notes app, spreadsheet, or budgeting app.

How to Set Up Sinking Funds

1. **Identify Your Categories:** Think about expenses you know will come up throughout the year. Common categories include:

   ❖ Travel

   ❖ Car maintenance

   ❖ Holiday shopping

   ❖ Medical co-pays

   ❖ Pet care

   ❖ Tech upgrades

   ❖ Annual insurance premiums

   ❖ Weddings or special events

2. **Estimate the Costs:** Figure out how much you'll need and by when.

   a. If holiday shopping will cost **$1,200** and you have *six months* to save, that's **$200** *per month.*

   b. If your pet's annual vet visit costs **$300**, that's **$25** *per month.*

3. **Automate Your Savings:** Set up automatic transfers from your checking to your savings on payday. Automation makes saving effortless and keeps you consistent. If your finances are unpredictable, set calendar reminders instead to check in and adjust based on what you can afford.

For example, let's say December was rough on your finances, so you set a monthly reminder for the first of each month to log into your banking app and take ten minutes to move some money around at your discretion. You have travel goals for this new year!

❖ In January, you decided to move $20 into your emergency fund and $10 into your "vacation" sinking fund.

❖ In February, you've recovered (a bit?) from the holiday spending and moved $30 into your emergency fund and moved $10 more into your sinking fund.

Not only does this get you into the habit of checking your bank accounts regularly, but it puts you in control of what needs to be changed or moved.

Sinking Fund Set Up Template

Category	Total Needed	Due Date	Monthly Goal	Where You're Saving It
Car Maintenance	$600	July 1	$100	HYSA—"Car" Subaccount
Dream Trip Fund	$2,500	Sept 15	$210	HYSA—"Vacation"
Holiday Gifts	$1,000	Dec 1	$100	HYSA—"Holidays"

Let's bring in Marisol, our first-gen *hermana* juggling family responsibilities, career moves, and financial glow-ups. She's been working hard to build her savings, but she *hates* feeling caught off guard by big expenses. So, she starts setting up sinking funds to help her get ahead.

Example 1: Marisol's Car Woes

Marisol's used car has been reliable, but she knows that an oil change and some brake work are coming up in about six months. The estimate? Around $600. Instead of waiting until the last minute and putting it on a credit card, she starts a car maintenance sinking fund.

❖ She decides to save $100 a month for six months.

❖ She sets up an automatic transfer from her checking to her savings every payday.

❖ When the repair bill hits, she pays it stress-free. No credit card debt, no anxiety.

Boom. Responsible *and* unbothered.

Example 2: The Family Christmas Dilemma

Every holiday season, Marisol wants to spoil her younger siblings and get her *mamá* something special. Last year, she waited until December and ended up charging everything to her credit card. This year? Not happening.

❖ She estimates she'll need $1,000 for gifts and travel.

❖ She sets aside $100 per month starting in February.

❖ By the time Black Friday deals hit, she already has the cash. No stress, no last-minute panic.

Sinking funds = making future Marisol's life easier.

Example 3: The Dream Trip Fund

Marisol has always wanted to take her *mamá* on a trip to Colombia to visit family. Flights, food, and fun will cost around $2,500. Instead of waiting until the last minute or putting it on a credit card, she sets up a travel fund.

❖ She gives herself a year to save and breaks it down into $210 per month.

❖ She gets a HYSA so her money earns a little interest while she saves.

❖ When it's time to book flights, she's ready—without the guilt or financial stress.

Moving money to your savings account is easier than you think. If your direct deposit goes into your checking account, log into your banking app and set up a recurring transfer to your sinking fund categories. Many banks and credit unions let you nickname your accounts, so you can label one "Travel Fund" or "Holiday Shopping" to keep things organized. The same can be said for emergency funds, so it's easier to identify which one is the priority "bucket" and which one is for that upcoming trip. HYSAs are particularly great for this because they let your money grow with interest, even while it's sitting there waiting for its purpose.

A sinking fund and emergency fund are really just fancy terms for savings with a purpose. Unlike an emergency fund, which is a safety net for unexpected events, sinking funds act like buckets or vaults for predictable expenses. They're ways to give every dollar a job. And yes, they can all live under one savings account if you want, divided mentally, on a spreadsheet, or labeled within your bank account.

Building an emergency fund and sinking funds takes time, but the peace of mind they bring is priceless. They're not just financial tools; they're acts of self-care and empowerment. Start small, stay consistent, and remember that every dollar saved is a step toward a more secure future.

CHAPTER 5

THE PROS AND CONS OF HIGH-YIELD SAVINGS ACCOUNTS

"Quien con lobo se junta, a aullar aprende."

Money habits are contagious.

Quien con lobo se junta, a aullar aprende... The people and institutions you associate with will shape your financial mindset and journey.

If you park your savings in a traditional bank with a 0.01% interest rate, your money is essentially sitting there doing nothing. But if you align yourself with banks that prioritize growth, like SoFi, Ally, Marcus by Goldman Sachs, and many more, you start playing the game differently. You're learning to make your money work for you instead of just working for your money.

High-yield savings accounts (HYSAs) are a financial game-changer, especially for anyone looking to make their money work harder. Digital banks like the ones mentioned above and many others offer these accounts with interest rates that far surpass those of traditional banks like BOA, Chase, or Wells Fargo. One of their most appealing features, besides the higher interest rates, is the ability to organize your funds into subcategories or "money vaults," as mentioned in the previous chapter. These vaults can be labeled for specific goals, such as emergency funds, vacations, or future car repairs, making your financial intentions visually clear and motivating. The best part? You can still access these funds whenever you want, just like a checking account, unlike an investment account.

HYSAs stand out because they're all about earning. Imagine you're saving for your "June Vacation" sinking fund, collectively holding $5,000, and you park that money in a HYSA earning 4% annual interest. That's $200 of free money in just one year, simply for being intentional about where you store your savings. Over time, thanks to the magic of compound interest, your savings grow exponentially.

How Your $5,000 Grows Over Five Years

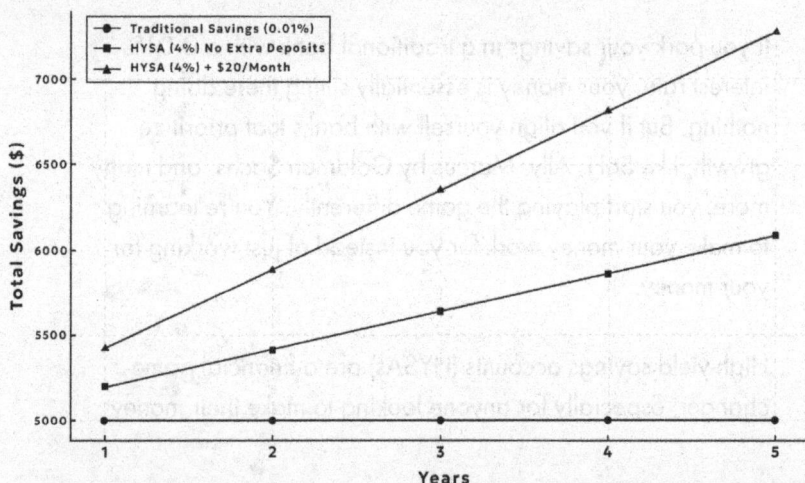

Of course, HYSAs aren't without their minor drawbacks...
but hear me out! The interest you earn is considered taxable
income, which means you'll pay taxes on it come tax season.
While this might sound like a downside, the benefits far
outweigh the cons. Even after taxes, the interest you earn still
surpasses what you'd get from a traditional savings account
offering 0.01% interest, where your $5,000 would earn a
meager 50 cents in a year.

Interest Earned in One Year on $5,000

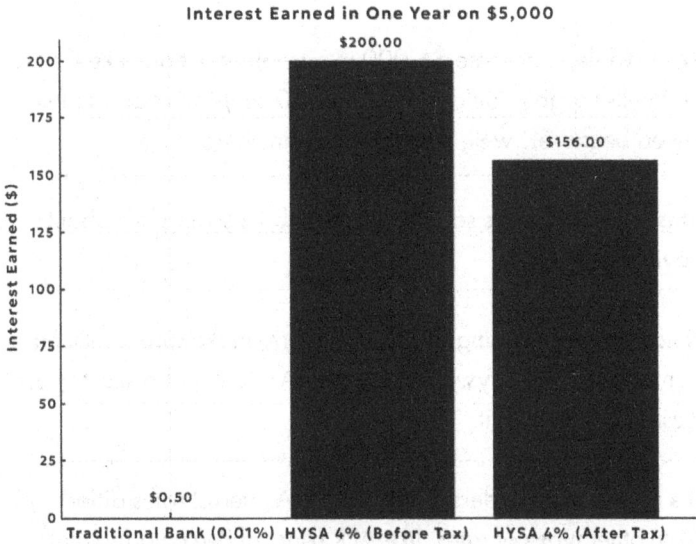

Even after taxes, the difference is night and day:

* ❖ Traditional bank interest (0.01%) = $0.50
* ❖ HYSA interest (4%) = $200 before tax, $156 after tax
    (assuming a 22% tax rate)

This graph shows why where you keep your money matters.
A traditional savings account gives you literal pocket change,

while a HYSA helps your money actually grow, even when you factor in taxes.

Let's break it down:

If you earned $200 in interest from your HYSA and you're in the 22% tax bracket, you'd owe around $44 in taxes. That still leaves you with $156 of free money, just for letting your savings sit and earn.

Meanwhile, that same $5,000 in a traditional bank like Chase or Wells Fargo? You'd make about 50 cents all year. No tax owed because…well, there's barely anything to tax.

This is why I always say: it's not just about saving. It's about saving smarter.

If your money is going to sit somewhere, make sure it's sitting somewhere that pays you back. HYSAs don't just protect your cash. They elevate it.

It's important to understand how HYSA interest rates differ from other types of rates, like APR (Annual Percentage Rate) or credit card interest. The rate you see on a HYSA is an APY (Annual Percentage Yield), which represents how much your money will grow over a year, including the effects of compounding. In contrast, APR on a credit card is the rate you're charged for borrowing money. While APY works in your favor by growing your savings, APR works against you by increasing what you owe. This distinction is crucial for recognizing the benefits of saving in a HYSA versus carrying debt on a high-interest credit card.

If you've experienced financial insecurity, having a significant amount of money in a savings account can feel like a safety blanket. That's valid. A well-stocked HYSA, like six to twelve months of expenses saved, can help alleviate money-related anxiety, offering a sense of control and preparedness. However, once you've addressed those emotional needs, it's worth considering if holding too much cash in savings is the best long-term strategy.

For those with a healthier relationship with money, the next step might involve reallocating some of those savings toward investments or retirement accounts. For example, instead of letting $20,000 sit in a savings account, you could put a portion into a Roth IRA. For first-generation children of immigrants, this might even extend to building retirement funds for parents who weren't familiar with these options. Imagine opening a Roth IRA for your *mamá*, setting her up for a more secure future, and showing her how financial systems work in her favor.

While HYSAs are fantastic for medium-term savings, they're just one piece of the puzzle. If your goal is to grow wealth over decades, investments will play a critical role, a topic we'll explore in depth in Chapter 10. For now, know that a HYSA is a powerful stepping stone to financial security and empowerment. It gives your money a purpose and helps you build momentum for larger financial goals.

CHAPTER 6

LET'S TALK TAXES (WITHOUT THE PANIC)

"El miedo no anda en burro."

Fear moves fast, but understanding moves smarter. *El miedo no anda en burro*, my *abuela* used to say. Fear doesn't take its time. It shows up fast and uninvited, especially when we're dealing with things we were never taught, like taxes. But once we slow down and break it down? That fear starts to shrink. We take the power back, one concept at a time.

Taxes get a bad rap. I get it. For many of us, the word alone brings flashbacks of paperwork, panic, and Googling "What is a W-2" at 11:59 p.m. on April 14. But as overwhelming as taxes can feel, they're not something to fear once you understand the basics.

So, let's break it down together...without the shame, the panic, or the jargon.

What Even Gets Taxed?

Here are a few common things that get taxed in the US:

- ❖ Your paycheck (a.k.a. earned income)
- ❖ Business income or freelance work
- ❖ Unemployment income
- ❖ Tips, bonuses, and commissions
- ❖ Interest earned (like from HYSAs)
- ❖ Dividends or investment gains
- ❖ Side hustles, Venmo payments for services, etc.

Yes, even your HYSA earnings are taxable. If your savings earn $10 in interest this year, the IRS sees that as "income," and it gets added to your total at tax time.[3]

But don't panic…it's taxed based on your *income bracket*.

What Are Tax Brackets?

Think of tax brackets as a layered cake. The more income you make, the more layers you add and each layer has its own tax rate.

---

3   "About Form 1099-INT, Interest Income," U.S. Internal Revenue Service, last modified June 6, 2025, www.irs.gov/forms-pubs/about-form-1099-int.

Here are the different tax brackets for 2025 as listed in an article by the IRS:[4]

"For tax year 2025, the top tax rate remained 37% for individual single taxpayers with incomes greater than $626,350 ($751,600 for married couples filing jointly). The other rates were:

- ❖ 35% for incomes over $250,525 ($501,050 for married couples filing jointly)

- ❖ 32% for incomes over $197,300 ($394,600 for married couples filing jointly)

- ❖ 24% for incomes over $103,350 ($206,700 for married couples filing jointly)

- ❖ 22% for incomes over $48,475 ($96,950 for married couples filing jointly)

- ❖ 12% for incomes over $11,925 ($23,850 for married couples filing jointly)

- ❖ 10% for incomes $11,925 or less ($23,850 or less for married couples filing jointly)"

So, if you earn $60,000, here's how it breaks down:

- ❖ The first $11,925 is taxed at 10%

- ❖ The next chunk, from $11,926 to $48,475, is taxed at 12%

- ❖ The remaining income, from $48,476 to $60,000, is taxed at 22%

4   U.S. Internal Revenue Service, *IRS Releases Tax Inflation Adjustments for Tax Year 2025*, (Washington: IRS, 2024), www.irs.gov/newsroom/irs-releases-tax-inflation-adjustments-for-tax-year-2025.

Only that last slice of your income is taxed at the higher rate. That's your *marginal tax rate*.

The *effective tax rate*, what you actually pay across the board, is much lower, probably around 14–16%, depending on your deductions and credits.

TLDR: You're not being punished for earning more. You're just paying a little more on the top layer, not the whole cake. Also, getting taxed more means you're actually earning more. Mindset, babe!

Wait...But Can I Lower My Taxable Income?

Here's where things get interesting. You can lower your taxable income *legally* by contributing to things like:

- ❖ **Traditional 401(k)** or **IRA** → Retirement contributions that reduce your taxable income now.

- ❖ **HSA (Health Savings Account)** → If you have a high-deductible health plan, you can stash pre-tax money here.

- ❖ **Self-employed?** → You can deduct business expenses like home office costs, software, and equipment.

You can also use a tax software or work with a tax preparer to identify deductions and credits (child tax credit, education credits, etc.) that lower your bill.

Let's say your total taxable income is $55,000. You earned $200 in HYSA interest and contributed $3,000 to a traditional IRA.

- ❖ Your income drops to **$52,000** for tax purposes.

- ❖ You *still* earned interest and took advantage of compound growth.

- ❖ You lowered your tax liability and potentially qualified for a refund or owed less.

That's strategy, *hermana*. That's alignment. You don't have to love taxes, but you *can* learn how to navigate them with confidence.

The truth is the US tax system wasn't built keeping in mind the melting pot of cultures and people that make up our beautiful population. But that doesn't mean we can't learn how to work it in our favor. Especially as first-gen women and children of immigrants, understanding taxes isn't just financial literacy— it's financial power.

We're not trying to become CPAs (or maybe you are!), but the idea is to understand enough to save more, keep more, and build more. Because once you're no longer afraid of tax season, you're that much closer to building generational wealth with clarity and peace of mind.

The Rich Hermana's Tax Cheat Sheet

Because we love clarity, not chaos.

Taxable Income

Money the IRS sees as income and wants a cut of. This includes wages, freelance pay, tips, interest from savings, side hustle income, etc.

W-2

A tax form your employer sends you at the end of the year. It shows how much you earned and how much was withheld in taxes. If you have a regular job with a paycheck, you'll get one of these.

1099

A tax form for independent contractors, freelancers, and side hustlers. No taxes are taken out, so you're responsible for paying them yourself.

HYSA (High-Yield Savings Account)

A savings account that earns more interest than a traditional bank account. The interest you earn is taxable, but still totally worth it.

Tax Brackets

The levels (or layers) of income that get taxed at different rates. The more you earn, the higher the rate on the *top portion* of your income.

Marginal Tax Rate

The rate applied to the *last dollar* you earned. If you're in the 22% tax bracket, that's your marginal rate (but not all your income is taxed at that rate).

Effective Tax Rate

Your *average* tax rate across all your income. This is usually lower than your marginal rate.

Standard Deduction

A fixed amount the IRS lets you subtract from your income before calculating taxes. In 2025, the standard deduction and married persons filing separately, $22,500 for a head of household, and $30,000 for a married couple filing jointly and surviving spouses.

Deduction vs. Credit

- ❖ **Deduction** reduces your *taxable income.*
- ❖ **Credit** reduces your *actual tax bill* dollar for dollar. *Credits are the real MVPs.*

401(k)

A retirement savings account offered by some employers. Contributions lower your taxable income now. Grows tax-deferred until retirement.

IRA (Individual Retirement Account)

A retirement account you open yourself.

- ❖ **Traditional IRA:** Contributions lower your taxable income now.
- ❖ **Roth IRA:** You pay taxes upfront, and then it grows tax-free forever (we love her).

HSA (Health Savings Account)

A triple-tax-advantaged account for healthcare savings. Must have a high-deductible health plan. Money goes in tax-free, grows tax-free, and comes out tax-free for qualified medical expenses.

Withholding

The money your employer takes out of your paycheck for taxes. You'll see this on your pay stub as "federal withholding" and possibly state too.

Estimated Taxes

Quarterly tax payments you make if you're self-employed or a side hustler and no one's withholding for you. Yes, even your Etsy shop may need these.

You got this, *hermana*. Taxes can be complicated, but you're not doing it alone and you're already miles ahead just by reading this.

CHAPTER 7

GETTING YOUR LIFE TOGETHER, ONE STICKY NOTE AT A TIME

"Haz bien y no mires a quién."

You're going to forget it. Start writing things down and setting reminders.

Life comes at you fast. Between work, family, social obligations, and the endless stream of notifications on your phone, it can feel like there's never enough time to get everything done. Add money management to the mix, and it's easy to see how things slip through the cracks. That's why staying organized isn't just a nice-to-have: it's an essential. When you set yourself up with systems that work for you, you're not just clearing mental clutter but setting the stage for financial and personal success.

That said, I want to acknowledge that staying organized, especially when it comes to finances, isn't equally easy for everyone. For people with ADHD, executive dysfunction, depression, or anxiety, managing money can feel like an uphill battle. Studies have shown that conditions like ADHD can impact working memory, time management, and impulse control, making it harder to keep track of bills, stick to budgets, or plan long-term. Research also links depression and anxiety to avoidance behaviors, which can lead to procrastination around financial tasks. If this sounds familiar, know that you're not alone, and it's not a personal failing. The key is to find strategies that work with your brain, not against it, like automating bill payments, setting calendar reminders, or using visual cues to stay on top of financial goals. Small tweaks can make a big difference in creating a system that supports you.

This chapter is about more than color-coded planners and calendar apps (though those are amazing). It's about creating a life where you feel in control, not overwhelmed. It's about healing old wounds, rebuilding your relationship with money, and making space for the goals you're chasing.

Many of us grew up watching our parents struggle with money. For immigrant families, those struggles were magnified by the challenges of navigating a foreign system. I mean, think about it. Your parents probably left everything behind to pursue a better future and, upon arriving, were suddenly responsible for bills, contracts, and financial paperwork in a language they barely understood. The stress was visible, and you likely felt it as their child.

You may have served as the family translator at ten years old, calling customer service or explaining legal documents to your parents. If you went to college, you probably had to figure out that whole process alone. These experiences shaped how you view money today. They may have instilled a sense of responsibility, but they also may have left you feeling anxious, unprepared, or resentful.

(Not So) Fun Fact

If you avoid opening emails or snail mail because you're afraid of what's inside, you're not alone. This is actually a widespread experience. This phenomenon, often referred to as "email anxiety," extends beyond digital communication to traditional mail as well. Psychologist Kia-Rai M. Prewitt, PhD, from the Cleveland Clinic, notes that email anxiety stems from our hyper-connected world, where the anticipation of messages can lead to stress and avoidance behaviors.[5] Similarly, *Psych Central* highlights that email anxiety involves feelings of stress or unease related to managing emails, which can manifest as avoidance behaviors, such as not checking or opening them.[6]

Now, combine that with the survival tactics you picked up as a kid…learning to stay quiet when bills were being discussed, watching your parents dodge calls from unknown numbers, or feeling their stress over money like it was your own. It makes sense that financial paperwork, statements, or bills

---

5   "How to Deal with Email Anxiety," Cleveland Clinic, August 20, 2021, health.clevelandclinic.org/email-anxiety.

6   Chantelle Pattemore, "All About Email Anxiety," PsychCentral, October 18, 2022, psychcentral.com/anxiety/email-anxiety.

trigger something deep in you. It's not your fault. But it *is* your responsibility to unlearn those habits. Healing begins with acknowledging how your upbringing influences your present relationship with money.

Planning: The Unseen Superpower

In Chapter 4, we followed Marisol as she built her emergency and sinking funds. But there was a deeper thread running through her story beyond just opening a HYSA: the subtle art of planning ahead.

Marisol wasn't just saving randomly. She had a plan. She anticipated expenses, prepared for unexpected costs, and set up systems to make sure she could handle financial curveballs without stress. That's the real magic of financial organization: it gives you a sense of control over your future instead of constantly reacting to emergencies.

Planning isn't about having every detail figured out; it's about giving yourself options. It's knowing that in the future you won't have to scramble for cash when your car breaks down or stress over a surprise bill. It's recognizing that structure isn't a burden, but a form of self-care.

Haz bien y no mires a quién.

You were probably raised hearing this phrase, which loosely translates to "Do good, no matter who's watching." You've likely lived by it...helping your family, translating documents, figuring out financial systems alone. But here's the thing: it's time to extend that same grace to yourself. Taking control of your money and setting up systems that make your life easier isn't just for other people's benefit anymore. It's for you. You deserve ease just as much as anyone else.

This is about making money management something that works for you instead of something you feel like you're constantly running from. Organization isn't about being perfect; it's about removing unnecessary stress so you can focus on what really matters: building the kind of financial future that allows you to thrive.

Think about it. When was the last time you were in a mental funk and decided to declutter? You probably quickly realized that clearing up the space around you made way for new ideas and motivation to flow seamlessly. The same concept applies to financial organization. When you set up a system, even a simple one, you free up mental energy that can be used for bigger goals, rather than constantly playing catch-up with your money.

So, how do you start?

The key is to find systems that fit your brain rather than forcing yourself into a one-size-fits-all approach. Here are some simple ways to make money management easier:

- ❖ **Automate everything you can:** Set up autopay for bills, schedule recurring transfers to savings, and use reminders for due dates. If remembering to check statements is hard, let your bank send alerts.

❖ **Use the "two-minute rule":** If a financial task (like checking your account balance or opening a bill) takes less than two minutes, do it immediately to avoid procrastination.

❖ **Go visual:** If digital reminders don't work for you, try physical cues like sticky notes, a grocery budget tracker on your fridge, or a whiteboard with key due dates in your bedroom. Seeing your to-dos might feel overwhelming at first, but trust me. Waking up to a clear plan is way less stressful than waking up to a missed deadline.

❖ **Batch financial tasks:** Set a "money date" with yourself or your partner once a month to review your spending, pay bills, and check in on your goals. Making it a routine helps it feel like a normal part of life instead of something to dread. Why not make it enjoyable? Grab your favorite snacks, get comfy, and set the mood, because financial check-ins don't have to be stressful.

❖ **Find an accountability system:** Whether it's a budgeting buddy, a finance app that tracks your habits, or a simple checklist, having structure makes staying on top of money less stressful.

Take five minutes to set up one small system that makes money management easier for you today. Whether it's a bill reminder in your phone, a sticky note on your mirror, or a quick check of your account balance, start with one step. Small actions add up to big change.

CHAPTER 8

HEALING AND REBUILDING YOUR RELATIONSHIP WITH MONEY

"DeBÍ TiRAR MáS FOToS."

Your relationship with money wasn't built in a day, and healing it won't happen overnight, either. But here's the good news: you don't need to scrap everything and start over from scratch. Think of it like renovating a home. You don't bulldoze the whole thing just because one part needs work. You assess, repair, and rebuild.

Question for you: if money were a person, how would you describe your relationship?

Awkward and distant? A little toxic? Or full-on ghosting?

No matter where you're at, this chapter will help you move toward a relationship with money that feels supportive and empowering. Your job right now? Have grace with yourself. Forgive past mistakes. Set boundaries. Celebrate even the smallest wins...because every step counts.

Step 1: Reflect on Your Money Story

Your money story is like the background music of your financial life. It's always been there, quietly shaping how you think, feel, and act around money. The question is: *what's the vibe?* Is it upbeat and empowering, or does it make you feel overstimulated and unfocused?

This is why we started this book with the purpose path exercise. Feel free to revisit Chapter 1 whenever you need to.

Take a moment to reflect on where it all began. What were your earliest memories of money? Did your parents argue about it? Did you hear, *"Eso está muy caro"* or *"No hay dinero pa' eso"*? Maybe you learned to stretch every dollar or felt guilty asking for anything extra.

Whatever your story is, *honor it*. It's not about judgment; it's about understanding.

Write down three beliefs about money that you grew up with. Then, ask yourself: do these beliefs serve me today?

Step 2: Forgive Yourself and Others

We've all made money mistakes—yes, even the most "together" people. The difference? They don't let those mistakes define them. For many first-gen kids, we also carry the weight of what our families couldn't do: the opportunities they didn't have, the sacrifices they made. That's a lot to hold.

But guilt and resentment? They're like financial quicksand. They keep you stuck.

Self-compassion research shows that forgiving yourself can ease emotional burdens and help you move forward.[7]

So, here's your permission slip to let go:

- ❖ *Forgive* yourself for not knowing what you didn't know.

- ❖ *Forgive* past mistakes: the credit card debt, the impulse purchases, the financial avoidance.

- ❖ *Forgive* your parents for what they couldn't teach you. They were surviving. Now, you're learning to thrive.

I won't lie. I'm still salty about that coworker who never paid me back the $10 I loaned them on a work trip. But I also know that marinating in bitterness doesn't serve me. Part of breaking generational money trauma is learning to release, not ruminate.

---

7 Kristin D. Neff and Marissa C. Knox, "Self-Compassion," in *Encyclopedia of Personality and Individual Differences*, ed. V. Zeigler-Hill and T. K. Shackelford (Springer International Publishing AG, 2017).

Write a letter of forgiveness to yourself or someone else. You
don't have to send it. Just putting the words on paper can
be freeing.

Step 3: Educate Yourself (But Make It Fun)

Personal finance is a skill, not an innate talent. No one is born
knowing how to budget, save, or invest. While you might not
have learned this in school or through your family, it's never too
late to become a self-taught Rich Hermana with her life on track.

The key? Make it easy and doable. Start small and keep it
consistent. Whether it's listening to a podcast on your commute
or reading one chapter of a finance book on Sundays, every
bit of knowledge you gain is a way to embrace a newfound
appreciation and enjoyment toward money management.

Yes...working on your finances *can* be fun, especially when
you realize that it'll buy you time, experiences, and peace.

Choose one finance topic you want to learn more about this
month (budgeting, investing, credit scores) and set aside
twenty minutes a week to focus on it. If staying focused feels
like a struggle, try the Pomodoro Method: work on one thing
for twenty-five minutes, then take a five-minute break to stretch,
sip water, or just breathe. After four rounds, take a longer
fifteen- to thirty-minute break. It's a gentle way to learn in small,
stress-free bites...perfect for those moments when life feels full.
Put your phone on Do Not Disturb.

This is your time. For *you*.

Step 4: Set Boundaries (Without the Guilt)

As a first-gen child of immigrants, you've probably felt the tension of wanting to help your family while also building your own life. The truth is you can't pour from an empty cup, and gone are the days of loaning your cousin a few dollars here and there without knowing when you'd get that money back...if ever.

Setting boundaries doesn't mean you don't care. It means you're making sure you're in a position to help long-term by putting your finances and needs first. Start by identifying what feels overwhelming. Is it financial support? Emotional labor? Then decide what limits work for you.

It's okay to say, "I can help with X, but I *can't* do Y right now." You're not being selfish; you're being sustainable.

Think of boundaries as love in action. You're protecting your future so you can show up for yourself and your family in a way that doesn't burn you out. Practice one boundary this week. Maybe it's declining a request for money or saying no to a favor that drains you. Make sure to celebrate the fact that you're prioritizing your well-being by adding it to a "gratitude" checklist on your notes app or sticky note.

Step 5: Automate Your Finances

Automation isn't just a convenience; it's a game-changer. Imagine this: your bills are paid on time, your savings grow steadily, and you don't even have to think about it. That's the magic of automation. It takes the guesswork (and stress) out of money and life management.

Start small. Set up autopay for one bill or a recurring transfer to your savings account. Over time, you can automate more, like investments or sinking funds for big goals. The less you have to rely on willpower or brainpower, the better.

Think of automation as your financial assistant working behind the scenes. You're freeing up mental space to focus on bigger things like that dream vacation or starting a side hustle.

Today, log into your bank account and set up one automatic payment or transfer. You'll thank yourself later.

Step 6: Celebrate Your Progress

Healing your relationship with money is a journey, and every step deserves recognition. Maybe you finally stuck to your budget for the first time, opened a HYSA, or had a conversation about money without spiraling into anxiety.

These aren't just minor wins; they're powerful indicators that you're shifting your mindset and building confidence.

Progress isn't about perfection. It's about consistency.

And when you celebrate your small wins, you reinforce those positive financial habits, making it easier to stay on track. Too often, we dismiss our progress because we think we should be further along. But here's the truth: financial growth goes beyond saving and investing. It's also diving deep into how you *feel* about money.

If you're less anxious when checking your bank account, *that's progress.*

If you're saying no to impulse purchases that don't align with your goals, *that's growth.*

If you're no longer avoiding financial conversations out of fear, *that's a huge transformation.*

Acknowledging these shifts helps you build confidence, and confidence is what keeps you going. Imagine looking back in a year and seeing all the tiny steps that added up to massive change. That's the power of celebrating along the way.

So, how do you make sure you actually recognize your progress? Write it down.

Keep a running list of financial wins in a notebook, your notes app, or a dedicated finance journal. It can be as small as "paid my bills on time" or as big as "hit my savings goal this month." When you have moments of doubt or feel like you're not doing enough, looking back at your wins will remind you that *you are moving forward.*

And don't just track progress. Celebrate it.

Like Bad Bunny once said, *"DeBÍ TiRAR MáS FOToS."* It's so easy to move fast that we forget to document our journey, to look back and actually see how far we've come. But just like you'd want to capture memories from a life-changing trip or a major milestone, you should also document your financial wins, big and small.

❖ Take a screenshot when you hit a savings goal.

❖ Write down the first time you paid a bill in full without stress.

❖ Log the moment you chose financial peace over guilt.

Because one day, you'll look back at these "photos" of your progress and realize how much your mindset and habits have transformed.

No matter where you're starting, remember that you're not behind. You're right where you need to be to begin healing and building a better future. One step at a time. You've got this.

A Rich Hermana Tip

Staying on top of your finances goes beyond budgeting. It's about staying on top of your life as a whole. When you're organized, you remove unnecessary stress and create space for financial clarity. Simple tools, like calendar reminders for bill payments, a running to-do list in your phone's notes app, or sticky notes with motivational quotes around your work space can keep you focused and accountable.

Project management isn't just corporate jargon. It's a mindset that can help you stay on top of your financial life.

Personally, I rely on tools like Notion, Asana, AirTable, Google Drive, and Monarch to track expenses, organize important documents, and plan long-term goals. You don't need to master every app or dive down a rabbit hole trying to find the perfect system. The goal isn't to overwhelm yourself with tech, it's to find what works for you and stick with it. Whether it's a simple notes app or a full-blown spreadsheet setup, the best system is the one you'll actually use.

CHAPTER 9

MONEY AND RELATIONSHIPS

"Cuentas claras, amistades largas."

Good fences make good neighbors.

If there's one thing that can turn a loving relationship into a telenovela-level drama, it's money. Whether it's with family, a romantic partner, or friends, financial misunderstandings can stir up guilt, resentment, and awkwardness faster than you can say, *"¿Y el dinero que te presté?"*

For many of us first-gens, money equals responsibility, loyalty, and sometimes, unspoken cultural expectations. If you've ever felt guilty for not sending enough money to your parents, struggled to set financial boundaries with a partner, or felt weird about splitting the bill with friends who "forget" their wallets, you're not alone. Money and relationships are deeply intertwined, and if we don't address them with clarity (*cuentas claras*), they can create tension in even the strongest connections.

Let's talk about how to navigate these money conversations with the people we care about while keeping both our wallets and our relationships intact.

Family: When Helping Becomes Expected

Growing up, many of us saw our parents sacrifice everything to give us better opportunities. Now that we're making money, it feels natural to want to give back. But what happens when generosity becomes an unspoken obligation?

Take Mariana, for example. The moment she got her first real paycheck, her mom casually mentioned that their light bill was due. Then her *tío* needed help fixing his car. Then her little cousin wanted a new laptop for school. Before she knew it, she was funneling half her paycheck into family expenses, and any attempt to say no was met with, *"¿Y para qué trabajas tanto entonces?"*

Sound familiar?

Helping our families is an act of love, but it shouldn't come at the cost of our own financial stability. The key is to set clear boundaries early on. Instead of waiting until you're overwhelmed, have an open conversation about what you can realistically contribute. For example, you might say: "I want to help, but I also need to build my own savings. I can commit to sending $100 a month, but beyond that, I won't be able to contribute."

By defining what's possible, you protect your own financial future while still honoring your values.

Romantic Relationships: Love Is Blind, but Your Bank Account Shouldn't Be

Money conversations in relationships can feel unromantic, but do you know what's even less romantic? Fighting over debt, overspending, or financial secrets.

Picture this: Sergio and Daniela have been dating for three years. They split rent, but whenever they go out, Sergio insists on paying. Daniela appreciates it but notices that Sergio gets stressed every time the bill arrives. Turns out, he's been putting everything on his credit card, thinking he has to "provide," even though they could easily afford to split things more evenly.

This is why financial transparency is so important. Before moving in together, making a big purchase, or even just establishing spending habits, it's crucial to ask:

❖ What are our financial goals as a couple?

❖ How do we feel about debt, savings, and lifestyle choices?

❖ How will we split expenses fairly (not just equally)?

There's no one right way to handle money in relationships, but the worst approach is avoiding the conversation entirely. Whether you keep separate accounts, combine everything, or do a mix of both, the key is being on the same page. *Cuentas claras, relaciones largas.*

Friendships: The "Let's Split It" Dilemma

Friendship and finances can be tricky, especially when everyone's at different income levels.

Say your friends love to do fancy brunches every weekend, but you're trying to save for a house. Do you go and spend money you don't want to? Or do you decline and risk feeling left out?

Or maybe you're the friend who's doing a little better financially, and you don't mind covering drinks sometimes... until it becomes an expectation.

The solution? *Be upfront.*

You don't have to overshare your financial situation, but a simple, "I'm on a budget right now, so I'm skipping brunch, but let's do a coffee date instead" sets the boundary without guilt. If you're the friend with more financial flexibility? Generosity is great, but it's okay to say no when it stops feeling fair.

True friends won't judge you for prioritizing your financial goals. If they do, well...maybe it's time to reevaluate that friendship.

At the end of the day, money will test our emotions, values, and expectations. The best way to keep financial stress from ruining your relationships is to talk about it openly and honestly.

So, the next time money and relationships collide, remember: *cuentas claras, amistades (y relaciones) largas.*

CHAPTER 10

TYPES OF INVESTMENTS

"No pongas todos los huevos en la misma canasta."

If there's one thing our immigrant parents drilled into us, it was the importance of saving: tucking money away under the mattress, keeping it in a savings account (even if it earns nothing), and never spending unless absolutely necessary. *Porque nadie sabe lo que va a pasar mañana.* And while that mindset may have helped them survive uncertainty, it won't help us build anything in the long run.

The truth is you can't save your way to wealth. Saving is just step one. It keeps your money safe, but it doesn't grow it. Investing, on the other hand, is what turns money into generational wealth. That's where the immigrant mindset often holds us back. Many of us grew up watching our parents work tirelessly, never trusting banks, and believing that risk equals danger. But, in reality, not investing is the bigger risk.

Think about it. Every year, inflation eats away at your savings. A $20 bill today won't buy what it did ten years ago, and it'll buy even less ten years from now. The wealthy understand this, which is why they don't just save…they invest wisely and diversify. As the saying goes, "*No pongas todos los huevos en la misma canasta.*" Don't put all your eggs in one basket.

The Importance of Diversifying Your Income Streams

We weren't taught this growing up, but relying on a single paycheck is one of the riskiest things you can do nowadays. If all your income comes from one job, one employer, or one source, you're one emergency away from financial struggle. Wealthy people don't just work for money. They make their money work for them.

Investing is a way to do that. It's about playing the long game, building multiple streams of income, and setting yourself up so that one day, you don't have to work for every dollar. It's not just about getting rich; it's about achieving work-life balance and having the time to spend with your family, travel, and enjoy life without worrying about money.

Another hard pill to swallow? Social Security won't be enough to retire on. Our parents may have believed that working hard until retirement meant financial security, but the reality is, by the time we retire, Social Security won't make a dent in our living expenses. The government isn't going to save us. We have to save *ourselves*.

So, how do we start? By investing correctly and getting educated. I'm not a financial professional, so I won't tell you what specific investments to make. But what I *will* do is help you understand the different types of investments so that you can make informed decisions and seek guidance from actual financial professionals when needed.

Types of Investments (From Lowest Risk to Highest Risk)

Not all investments are created equal. Some are safer, while others offer bigger potential returns but come with more risk. Here's a breakdown of common investment types, ranked from easiest and lowest risk to most complex and higher risk.

Index Funds & ETFs (Low Risk, Long-Term Growth)

If you're new to investing, index funds and ETFs (Exchange-Traded Funds) are one of the simplest ways to get started. They are collections of stocks or bonds that track the overall market, making them diversified by design.

- ❖ **Why they're great:** Instead of picking individual stocks (which is risky and time-consuming), you're investing in the entire market. Historically, the stock market grows over time even with short-term dips.

- ❖ **Why you need patience:** The key here is not touching that money. Investing in index funds is a *long-term game*. If you invest $100 a month consistently, in thirty years, that money could turn into six figures, depending on market growth.

❖ **Automation is your best friend:** Many people set up automatic investments, where money goes into their index fund every month without them having to think about it. *Set it and forget it.*

> ### A Rich Hermana Tip
>
> I opened my first investment account thinking I had to check it every day like a day trader. But once I set up automatic investments into an index fund, I learned that the real power is in *leaving it alone.* It's been years now, and I can already see my money growing without me doing a thing. Trust the process!

Retirement Accounts (Tax-Advantaged and Employer-Matched Money!)

Most of us never heard of 401(k)s or IRAs growing up because our parents never had them. But if your job offers a 401(k) with an employer match, you need to be taking advantage of it.

❖ **What's a 401(k)?** It's a retirement account that lets you invest money tax-free while you're working. Many employers match your contributions (for example, if you put in 5% of your paycheck, your employer might add another 5% for free). That's free money!

❖ **What's a Roth IRA?** It's a personal retirement account where you pay taxes now, but your money grows tax-free. That means when you retire, you don't owe Uncle Sam a dime on your investments.

❖ **Why they matter:** If you're not investing in these accounts, you're leaving thousands of dollars on the table.

A Rich Hermana Tip

I had no idea what a 401(k) was until my first corporate job when I was twenty-two. No one in my family talked about retirement accounts because they never had access to them. When I learned that my employer was offering free money through a 401(k) match, I maxed it out ASAP. If your job offers a match, don't leave free money on the table!

Here's how you can start investing today:

1. **Open a brokerage account:** Platforms like Vanguard, Fidelity, or Charles Schwab make it easy to start.

2. **Set up tax-advantaged accounts:** If your job offers a 401(k) match, contribute at least up to the match! Open a Roth IRA if you qualify.

3. **Automate your investments:** Set a monthly amount and let it grow.

4. **Educate yourself:** Follow finance professionals, read books, and seek professional advice if needed, especially when you're just starting out.

Real Estate (Higher Barrier to Entry, Potential Passive Income)

Buying property is a common way to invest, but it's not as easy as HGTV makes it look. It requires a lot of upfront capital, maintenance, and risk.

❖ **Why people invest in real estate:** Rental properties can provide passive income, meaning your tenants pay you every month.

❖ **What to watch out for:** It's not always "passive." Managing tenants, repairs, and market fluctuations can be stressful.

❖ **Alternative:** REITs (Real Estate Investment Trusts) let you invest in real estate without actually buying a property.

A Rich Hermana Tip

I once looked into buying a rental property, but after seeing all the hidden costs (maintenance, property taxes, potential bad tenants), I decided to invest in a REIT ETF instead. Now I get the benefits of real estate investing without dealing with leaky toilets.

Starting a Business (High Risk, Possible High Reward)

Many first-gen immigrants were raised by hustlers. Our parents found ways to make extra money selling food, cleaning houses, or running small side businesses. But starting a full-fledged business is another level of risk and commitment.

- ❖ **Why it's powerful:** Being your own boss means unlimited earning potential and financial freedom.

- ❖ **Why it's risky:** Not all businesses succeed, and it takes time and money to scale.

- ❖ **Online business boom:** Many people today start digital businesses (consulting, e-commerce, content creation) that have lower startup costs.

A Rich Hermana Tip

When I started The Rich Hermana, I didn't know if it would take off. But investing in myself with proper courses and mentorship helped me turn it into an actual business that started online with a very low startup cost. If you're thinking about starting something, start small and test your idea before going all in!

The goal is to build financial independence, so you can live life on your terms. Because we weren't meant to work until we're old. We were meant to thrive.

CHAPTER 11

CREDIT BUILDING = YOUR PASSPORT TO FINANCIAL FREEDOM

If you grew up in a cash-only household where credit cards were "for emergencies only" (or worse, a "trap" to avoid at all costs), I feel you. But let's get one thing straight. Credit isn't just about borrowing money. It's about proving you can be trusted with money. When you do that well, doors open, like:

❖ Renting an apartment

❖ Getting a car loan with a decent interest rate

❖ Qualifying for the best credit card perks (hello, travel points and cashback!)

❖ Even getting a job (some employers check credit reports!)

So, let's break it down.

Step 1: Getting Your First Credit Card (Without Fear)

Your first credit card is like a baby step into the credit world. Here's how to get started:

- ❖ **Start with a secured credit card:** You put down a deposit (like $200), and that becomes your credit limit. It's like training wheels for your credit score.

- ❖ **Ask to be an authorized user:** If your parents, sibling, or trusted friend has good credit, being added to their account can boost your score.

- ❖ **Look for student or starter credit cards:** If you're new to credit, some banks offer beginner-friendly options with lower limits.

- ❖ **Consider store cards or lines of credit:** Retailers like Best Buy, Macy's, Amazon, and PayPal offer credit lines with promotional financing (like 0% interest for twelve months). These can be a great way to build credit while making essential purchases, just as long as you have a plan to pay them off on time.

A Rich Hermana Tip

At nineteen, when I first started my photography business to make ends meet, I needed a new camera body, a lens, memory cards, and an external hard drive. It was *not* cheap. I was determined to upgrade my gear, but I didn't have the cash upfront since I was working a part-time job while going to school.

Best Buy offered me the best deal at the time: twelve months without accumulating interest since my total was over $1,000. I saw it as an opportunity, but I also knew that if I didn't pay it off in time, I'd get hit with all the back interest.

I made it my goal to pay it off before the twelve months were up by hustling extra hard with photoshoots. Every time I got paid for a gig, I put a chunk of it toward my Best Buy balance. By the time the twelve months ended, I had paid off the entire balance and, to my surprise, my credit score had jumped almost immediately.

That first line of credit was a lesson in financial responsibility. If you use store credit wisely (and with a solid payoff plan), it can be a great way to build credit without paying a cent in interest.

Step 2: Understanding Your Credit Score (No, It's Not a Mystery)

Your credit score is a three-digit number that tells lenders how risky (or responsible) you are. Here's what goes into it:

- ❖ **35%: Payment history** (Do you pay your bills on time?)

- ❖ **30%: Credit utilization** (How much of your credit limit are you using?)

- ❖ **15%: Length of credit history** (How long have you had accounts open?)

- ❖ **10%: Credit mix** (Do you have different types of credit, like a card and a loan?)

❖ **10%: New credit inquiries** (How often are you applying for new accounts?)

A common mistake is maxing out your credit card. You should aim to use *less than 30%* of your credit limit, and ideally *under 10%* for the best score while you still familiarize yourself with credit card utilization and payoff.

For example, if your limit is $1,000, keep your balance under $300 (but preferably under $100) each month.

Step 3: How Interest Rates Work (a.k.a. the Cost of Borrowing Money)

Interest rates are how banks make money off you. If you carry a balance on your credit card, you're charged an APR (Annual Percentage Rate). This is why paying off your balance *in full* every month is the move.

For example, if you have a $1,000 balance and a 25% APR, carrying that balance could cost you an extra $250 a year in interest. Ouch!

A Rich Hermana Tip

Listen, APR is a scam that banks *love* because it keeps you paying way more than you actually owe. Think of it as an extra tax on your future self, but one that you didn't vote for.

So, I reprogrammed my mindset around it. I started telling myself: "If I can't pay for this in cash or in full this month, I'm not swiping my card."

This simple rule changed *everything* for me. It forced me to be intentional with my spending, prioritize my needs over my wants, and most importantly, avoid handing banks my hard-earned money in interest.

If you buy a $100 pair of shoes on a credit card with 25% APR and only make the minimum payment, those shoes could end up costing you $130 or more. That's money you could've put toward savings, investing, or even another purchase you *actually* need.

So, before you swipe, ask yourself:

- ❖ Do I already have the cash to cover this?
- ❖ Will I be able to pay it off in full by the next due date?
- ❖ Is this purchase adding value to my life or just instant gratification?

If the answer is no to any of the above, *walk away*. Your future self will thank you.

Step 4: The Credit-Building Game Plan

Building credit is about managing it wisely so that your score grows consistently over time. Here's your Rich Hermana-approved blueprint for leveling up your credit without stress:

1. **Always Pay on Time (Autopay Is Your Bestie)**

   a. Payment history makes up 35% of your credit score, so missing a due date is a quick way to tank your progress.

   b. Even being one day late can trigger fees and a ding on your report.

   c. Set up autopay, or at least calendar reminders, so you never forget.

A Rich Hermana Tip

If money is tight, pay at least the minimum due to avoid late fees and protect your score. Then, throw extra payments at the balance when possible.

---

2. **Keep Your Balance Low (The 30% Rule Is the *Maximum*, Not the Goal!)**

   a. Your credit utilization (how much of your available credit you're using) makes up 30% of your score.

   b. The golden rule: keep your balance under 30% of your total limit. For the best score, aim for 10% or lower.

   c. For example, if you have a $1,000 limit, try not to let your balance go over $300. But if you can keep it under $100, even better.

   A Rich Hermana Tip

   If you've already swiped a big purchase and your balance is high, make a payment *before* your statement closes. This lowers your reported utilization and can boost your score faster.

3. **Don't Apply for Too Many Cards at Once (Slow and Steady Wins the Credit Race)**

   a. Every time you apply for a new credit card, it triggers a hard inquiry, which can lower your score by a few points.

   b. Multiple applications in a short time? That's a red flag to lenders that you might be desperate for credit.

   c. Spacing out your credit applications (every six to twelve months) is key.

A Rich Hermana Tip

If you get pre-approved offers, they don't impact your score until you formally apply. That's because most pre-approvals use a soft credit pull (a quick peek at your credit that doesn't leave a mark or lower your score). A hard pull (what happens when you actually apply) is what dings you a few points.

How to spot soft pull options? Think of those credit card offers you get in the mail saying, "You're pre-approved!" That's a soft pull. Online, look for phrases like "See if you pre-qualify" or "Check your rate without affecting your score". Always read the fine print before hitting "Apply".

4. **Check Your Credit Report for Mistakes (Because Errors Happen More Often Than You Think)**

   a. Credit bureaus make mistakes all the time, and you could be paying the price.

   b. A wrong late payment, an account you never opened, or a balance that's reported incorrectly? All of these can lower your score unfairly.

   c. Check your credit report for *free* at AnnualCreditReport.com every year.

A Rich Hermana Tip

If you find an error, dispute it ASAP with the credit bureau. They legally have to investigate and getting mistakes removed could bump up your score instantly.

Building credit is *not about spending more*, it's about
managing what you have *wisely*. Stick to this game plan,
and you'll watch your credit score climb, opening up bigger
financial opportunities in the future.

There's a saying: *"El crédito es como la reputación: se tarda
años en construir y un segundo en destruir."*

And it's true. You can spend years building up a solid credit
score, only to see it drop overnight because of one missed
payment or reckless spending. The good news? If you're
intentional, you can protect and grow your credit score like the
financial queen you are.

CHAPTER 12

DEBT PAYOFF METHODS THAT ACTUALLY WORK

"Más vale paso que dure, y no trote que canse."

Debt isn't the enemy. But interest? We don't like him.

Debt gets a bad rep, but let's be real: most of us didn't have a trust fund to cover college, cars, or even emergency expenses. Sometimes, debt is just part of the game. So, we might as well learn how to use it to our advantage like rich folks, *me entiendes?*

Interest. He's a sneaky little fee that turns a $5,000 loan into a $7,000 bill over time. If you don't have a plan, debt will eat away at your future wealth before you even get the chance to build it.

In this chapter, we're breaking down the best debt payoff methods, plus the mindset shifts you need to get out of the red and *stay* out.

Step 1: Know Your Numbers (a.k.a. Face the Music)

Before we talk strategy, you need to know exactly how much you owe (even if it makes you cry a little).

First, we'll start by making a list of:

- ❖ Every debt you have (credit cards, car loans, student loans, personal loans, etc.)

- ❖ The balance (how much you owe)

- ❖ The interest rate (because this determines how expensive your debt is)

- ❖ The minimum payment (so you know what you *must* pay each month)

If looking at your debt feels overwhelming, pour yourself a *cafecito*, play your favorite playlist, and treat this like a financial self-care moment. Because that's exactly what it is.

Step 2: Choose Your Payoff Strategy

In my experience, there are two tried-and-true ways to pay off debt. Let's start with the **Snowball Method**, made for quick wins and motivation. This one is best for people who need the extra push by seeing debts disappear fast, building momentum to keep you going.

- ❖ Step 1: Pay the minimum on all your debts.

- ❖ Step 2: Put *extra money* toward the *smallest debt* first.

- ❖ Step 3: Once that's paid off, roll that payment into the next smallest debt.

- ❖ Step 4: Repeat until you're debt-free!

Then there is my favorite, the **Avalanche Method**. This method helps you pay less in interest and get out of debt faster. This one is best for people who want to save hundreds or even thousands in interest by attacking high-cost debt first.

- ❖ Step 1: Pay the minimum on all your debts.

- ❖ Step 2: Put *extra money* toward the debt with the *highest interest rate* first.

- ❖ Step 3: Once that's paid off, roll that payment into the next highest-interest debt.

- ❖ Step 4: Repeat until you're debt-free!

If you're struggling to pick one, start with the Snowball Method for motivation. Once you get in the habit, you can switch to Avalanche to save more on interest.

Step 3: Cut Interest Costs (So You Pay Less Overall)

Interest is the toxic ex of your financial life—the kind that keeps showing up uninvited, draining your energy (and money), and making it impossible to move on. The longer interest sticks around, the harder it is to escape debt.

The key? *Cut it off ASAP.*

Tip 1: Call Your Credit Card Company and Ask for a Lower Rate

Yes, you *can* negotiate your APR! If you've been making on-time payments, many credit card companies will lower your interest rate if you just ask.

Here's what you can say: "Hi, I've been a responsible cardholder and always make my payments on time. I'd love to continue using this card, but my interest rate is too high. Can you lower it?"

They might say no, but they might say yes, and even a small drop in APR can save you hundreds.

Tip 2: Transfer Your Balance to a 0% Interest Credit Card

If your current card is charging 20%+ interest, look for a balance transfer card with a 0% APR intro period (usually twelve to eighteen months).

But read the fine print! Some balance transfers have fees, and the 0% APR only lasts for a limited time. The goal is to pay it off before interest kicks in.

Tip 3: Refinance Loans (If It Saves You Money)

Student loans, auto loans, and even personal loans can be refinanced to lower interest rates, meaning less money wasted and faster debt payoff.

Here's when refinancing makes sense:

- ❖ Your credit score has improved since you took out the loan.
- ❖ Interest rates have dropped.
- ❖ You can get a shorter loan term without a crazy high payment.

Now…here's when refinancing can be a bad idea:

- ❖ If you have federal student loans, refinancing could mean losing benefits like income-driven repayment or loan forgiveness.

Tip 4: Use Windfalls Wisely (Bonus Money = Debt Payoff Fuel)

Tax refund? Bonus from work? Side hustle cash? Instead of blowing it on a last-minute trip to Tulum (*I see you*), throw it at your highest-interest debt.

You have to treat interest like an ex that keeps texting you. It's draining, annoying, and stopping you from living your best life. The sooner you cut it off, the better.

Step 4: Find Extra Money to Throw at Your Debt

The faster you pay off debt, the less you'll spend on interest. Simple math. Here's how you might be able to free up extra cash:

Tip 1: Cut or Pause Unnecessary Subscriptions

Netflix, Hulu, Apple Music, Disney+...do you *really* need all of them? Even cutting just one for a few months can free up money to put toward debt.

Tip 2: Start That Side Gig

There's no need to work 24/7, but even an extra $100–$200 a month from a side gig can seriously speed up your debt payoff.

Tip 3: Use the "Spending Match" Rule

For every nonessential thing you buy (like that $50 late-night DoorDash order), match that amount toward debt. This forces you to be mindful about spending and can help speed up your payoff.

Step 5: Stay Debt-Free Once You Get There

Getting out of debt is one thing. *Staying* out is another. It's the whole reason why I started this book by tackling the mindset shift before diving into the numbers.

- ❖ **Tip 1:** Build that emergency fund. Aim for at least $1,500 to start, so unexpected expenses don't send you back into debt.

- ❖ **Tip 2:** Use credit like a tool, not a crutch. Only swipe your card if you can pay it off in full each month.

- ❖ **Tip 3:** Create a spending plan that works for you. Budgeting isn't about restriction, it's about being intentional with your money.

A Rich Hermana Tip

"Más vale paso que dure, y no trote que canse." Better a steady step that lasts than a sprint that exhausts. Debt payoff is a marathon, not a sprint. Some people burn themselves out trying to pay off debt overnight, then fall back into the same habits. The key is consistency by picking a method that works for you and sticking to it.

Because once you're debt-free? That's when the real wealth-building begins.

CHAPTER 13

NAVIGATING THE FINANCIAL SYSTEM FOR UNDOCUMENTED FAMILIES

Navigating the financial system is already complex, but for undocumented individuals and mixed-status families, it comes with an extra layer of challenges. From accessing banking services to building credit and financing education, undocumented individuals often face barriers that require creativity, persistence, and community support.

This chapter will break down key financial strategies, resources, and tips to help undocumented families thrive financially, even when traditional systems seem inaccessible.

Banking Without a Social Security Number

Many banks and credit unions require a Social Security Number (SSN) to open an account, but there are alternatives:

❖ **ITIN Accounts:** Some financial institutions allow individuals to open accounts using an Individual Taxpayer Identification Number (ITIN). The IRS issues ITINs regardless of immigration status.

❖ **Credit Unions & Immigrant-Friendly Banks:** Institutions like Self-Help Federal Credit Union and Latino Community Credit Union cater to immigrant communities and may have more flexible requirements.

❖ **Alternative Banking Methods:** Prepaid debit cards and mobile banking services (like Chime and Varo, among others) provide banking-like services without requiring an SSN.

Building Credit as an Undocumented Individual

Building credit is essential for financial stability, but without an SSN, the process can be tricky. Here's how undocumented individuals can start:

❖ **ITIN Credit Cards:** Some banks offer credit cards to ITIN holders. Institutions like Capital One and American

Express have been known to provide ITIN-based credit options.

- ❖ **Credit Builder Loans:** These small loans from credit unions or online lenders help establish credit while saving money.

- ❖ **Becoming an Authorized User:** A trusted family member or friend can add an undocumented person as an authorized user on their credit card, helping them build credit history.

Taxes and ITINs: Why Filing Matters

Undocumented individuals can (and should) file taxes using an ITIN. Filing taxes can:

- ❖ **Show Proof of Income** for rental applications or financial aid.

- ❖ **Help with Future Immigration Applications** (if policies change).

- ❖ **Qualify for Certain Tax Credits** (such as the Child Tax Credit, depending on the state).

To apply for an ITIN:

- ❖ Submit IRS Form W-7 along with tax documents.

- ❖ Use an IRS-authorized Certifying Acceptance Agent (CAA) for assistance.

❖ Check if local immigrant support organizations offer ITIN application help.

Entrepreneurship & Side Hustles: Making Money Without Traditional Employment

Since undocumented individuals often cannot legally work for an employer in the US, entrepreneurship and self-employment become powerful tools for financial stability:

❖ **Freelancing with an ITIN:** Platforms like Upwork, Fiverr, and Etsy allow users to earn income and report it under an ITIN.

❖ **Starting a Business:** Forming an LLC with an ITIN is possible in many states, allowing undocumented entrepreneurs to run legal businesses.

❖ **Cash-Based & Community Jobs:** Babysitting, cleaning services, mobile car wash, mobile grooming, landscaping, catering, and other informal work can be reliable income sources.

College & Financial Aid for Undocumented Students

While undocumented students are ineligible for federal financial aid, they may still have options:

- ❖ **State Financial Aid Programs:** Some states, like California (via the California DREAM Act), offer financial aid for undocumented students.

- ❖ **Private Scholarships:** Organizations like TheDream. US and MALDEF (Mexican American Legal Defense and Educational Fund) provide scholarships that do not require US citizenship.

- ❖ **University-Specific Funds:** Some schools have discretionary funds available for students regardless of immigration status. Talk to your financial aid office.

- ❖ **Graduate Fellowships & Research Stipends:** Some universities allow undocumented students to receive funding through nonemployment stipends or contractor arrangements using an ITIN.

Protecting Financial Security

Undocumented individuals are often targets for financial scams and exploitation. Here's how you can keep your family safe:

- ❖ **Avoid Notary Fraud:** Only licensed attorneys or DOJ-accredited representatives can provide legal advice.

- ❖ **Be Wary of Predatory Loans:** Some lenders exploit immigrant communities with high-interest payday loans. Stick to credit unions or community banks.

- ❖ **Know Your Rights:** Regardless of immigration status, everyone has the right to fair treatment in financial transactions.

Community Resources & Support

Several organizations offer financial education and support for undocumented families:

❖ **United We Dream** (unitedwedream.org): Advocacy and resources for undocumented youth.

❖ **Immigrant Legal Resource Center** (ilrc.org): Legal guidance for immigration-related financial matters.

❖ **TheDream.US** (thedream.us): Scholarships for undocumented students.

❖ **Self-Help Federal Credit Union** (self-helpfcu.org): Immigrant-friendly banking services.

While the financial system may not always be designed to support undocumented individuals, there are ways to build stability, create opportunities, and work toward financial goals for you and your loved ones. With the right knowledge, community support, and creative strategies, undocumented families can navigate financial barriers and work toward a more secure future.

If you or a loved one are undocumented, remember: financial empowerment is still possible, and you deserve the resources to thrive.

CHAPTER 14

NEGOTIATING YOUR WORTH

"El que no llora, no mama."

If there's one thing we weren't taught growing up, it's how to ask for more money, whether it's negotiating a starting salary, asking for a raise, or advocating for better benefits.

For many of us first-gens, the idea of negotiating feels… uncomfortable? We grew up watching our parents work extra hard just to get by, so the idea of walking into a boss's office and saying, "Actually, I deserve more" feels almost disrespectful and ungrateful.

But here's the truth: employers expect people to negotiate. And those who do? They make way more money over their careers than those who don't.

So, let's break the cycle. *No más "Gracias por la oportunidad, I'll take whatever you give me."* It's time to get that bag with confidence.

Step 1: Stop Settling for "Just Happy to Be Here"

Let's talk about Sofia. She was the first in her family to graduate from college and landed a solid marketing job right out of school. The salary? $55K.

She wanted to negotiate but felt guilty. *What if they take back the offer? What if they think I'm greedy?* So, she signed the contract and started working.

A year later, she found out a less experienced male coworker was making $65K.

Companies always have a range for what they're willing to pay. If they offer you the job, they want you. And unless you're applying for an extremely entry-level role, there's always room to negotiate.

Drop the "I'm lucky to be here" mindset and replace it with: "They're lucky to have me."

Step 2: Know Your Worth (With Receipts)

The strongest negotiations are based on facts, not feelings. Before you walk into that conversation, do your homework:

- ❖ **Market Research:** What's the industry standard for your role? Sites like Glassdoor, Payscale, and LinkedIn Salary Insights can give you a solid idea of what people in similar roles are making.

- ❖ **Company Research:** Is the company thriving? Did they just raise millions in funding? Are they actively hiring? These are signs they *can* afford to pay you more.

- ❖ **Your Receipts:** Whether you're negotiating a job offer or a raise, bring hard numbers on how you've contributed. Did you increase engagement by 50%? Bring in $100K in revenue? Save the company twenty hours a week with a new process? Numbers talk.

Once you have this info, set your number and aim higher than what you'd be happy with so you have room to negotiate.

Step 3: The Script That Gets You Paid

Let's say you're negotiating a job offer. Here's what you can say:

Them: "We're excited to offer you $65,000."

You: "I'm really excited about this opportunity, and I know I'd bring a lot of value to the team. Based on my experience and the industry standard, I'd like to discuss a salary closer to $75,000. Is there flexibility in the budget?"

Boom. You didn't demand anything... You just started
a conversation.

If they push back, don't panic. Companies rarely *immediately*
say yes. Instead, they might say:

❖ *"That's the max budget for this role."* → Ask about
  signing bonuses, additional paid time off (PTO), or
  education stipends instead.

❖ *"We reevaluate salaries after six months."* → Get that
  in writing before signing. They can casually "forget" on
  your next performance review in six months.

❖ *"We can do $70K, but not $75K."* → Congrats, you
  just made $5K more in five minutes.

If you're asking for a raise, follow the same approach but
highlight your contributions first:

You: "Over the last year, I've increased sales by 30%, led a
major project, and taken on additional responsibilities. Given
my impact, I'd like to discuss an increase to [$X]. How can we
make this happen?"

Step 4: Silence Is Your Superpower

Once you make your ask, shut up.

Seriously. Do not fill the silence.

Most people get nervous and start talking too much: "But if not, that's okay! I understand budgets! I'm just happy to be here!"

Don't do that. Employers expect negotiations, so let them respond. You're not being difficult. You're being strategic.

Step 5: Keep the Same Energy for Freelance & Side Hustles

Negotiating isn't just for nine-to-five jobs. If you're a freelancer, entrepreneur, or content creator, you should be charging what you're worth too.

If a client lowballs you, don't just say yes out of fear. Instead, say:

"I'd love to work with you, and my standard rate for this type of project is [$X]. Let me know how we can make this work!"

And if they hit you with "We don't have the budget"... *Cool. They're not your client.*

There's always someone willing to pay what you deserve. But you have to believe in your value first.

Advocate for yourself. *Siempre.* Negotiating isn't about greed; it's about being paid fairly for your skills, time, and expertise.

So next time you're nervous about asking for more, remember: employers expect it. The worst they can say is no (and you'll still have options). *El que no llora, no mama.* Those who don't make noise don't earn.

Now go get your money, *hermana.*

CHAPTER 15

PIVOT. *PIVOT!*

"El sol sale para todos."

Being locked into one career path for the rest of your life just doesn't sit right with me. Despite everything you were told in high school while being pressured to pursue higher education, the truth is that life will never be linear. Also, college in the United States is expensive AF.

In the same breath...honoring our immigrant parents' sacrifices by graduating with a degree is one of those unspoken agreements we as first-gen children task ourselves with. But here's something our parents were probably too afraid to do while surviving the trials and tribulations of living in a foreign country with limited opportunities and a language barrier: *pivoting.*

Financial success is not black and white. Although sometimes comfortable, relying on just one stream of income during times of financial crisis won't always lead to a stable life with low financial stressors. Sure, having a cushy, corporate job is the dream, and honestly a privilege nowadays, but no matter how much you love that job, someone higher up can easily decide to take it away from you, legally, and without explanation.

The economy is unpredictable. If you follow me on social media, you'll notice I never stop preaching the importance of figuring out how you can lock in multiple streams of income in today's world. If it's passive income, even better! It's not just about planning and building your safety net. It's realizing that it's a basic necessity nowadays.

The truth is that relying on a single paycheck will make you vulnerable to economic downturns, layoffs, and the whims of corporate restructuring.

Here's how I see it. Once you've diversified your income sources, you'll not only provide stability and security for your future self, but pave the first steps toward generational wealth. This can manifest in the form of freelancing, investing, or even starting a side business while letting your nine-to-five finance that dream.

As a multihyphenate, I took advantage of being unmarried and without children to go full force on every side hustle imaginable in my twenties. If it looked like it could keep me afloat from my underpaying nine-to-five, I was doing it. I was shooting weddings as a photographer on Friday nights after leaving my corporate job and using my weekends to freelance as a social media manager or shoot a family session at the park. I even dabbled in selling digital downloads and templates on Etsy for some additional passive income.

By cultivating various revenue streams, I created a buffer that protected me against unforeseen financial hardships and gave me greater peace of mind. I also have expensive taste, so no one was going to come save me from myself or that Prada bag.

During the day, I was a corporate baddie in marketing. At night, I was busy building a personal brand. My mother always liked to remind me of the importance of having a plan A through Z.

She would always say, "*El sol sale para todos,*" reminding me that there's enough success to go around, but only if you're willing to adapt and seize the opportunities in front of you.

I probably suffered from burnout one too many times in my twenties, but I was determined to support my family and have enough money to enjoy my weekends.

In an era where digital presence often also translates to professional opportunities, establishing a strong personal brand can also distinguish you from the crowd, and you better believe I took full advantage of this as a content creator in the early 2000s.

Ultimately, creating the life you deserve involves taking proactive steps to ensure your financial and professional independence. The earlier you do this, the better, but it also doesn't mean it's too late to pivot. Depending solely on a job that can easily lay you off or fire you at any moment ain't it, sis. If you like to live dangerously, that's wonderful, but I'm sure you wouldn't mind a little side of stability with your dessert.

The best day to start anything was yesterday. The next best day is today.

CHAPTER 16

THE ART OF MAKING MORE MONEY WITHOUT STARTING OVER

"Camarón que se duerme, se lo lleva la corriente."

There's more to life than just waiting for payday. If you have a spark, a skill, or a passion you want to bring to life outside of your job, there's some good news. Your nine-to-five can be more than a source of income. It can be the fuel to launch your dreams! A lot of us feel like we're stuck in the cycle of working just to pay bills, but what if you could use that steady paycheck to fund your *sueños*? Your job can be more than just income; it can be the *fuel* that helps you create the freedom to choose your own path.

The mistake a lot of us make is thinking we have to quit our jobs and take a giant leap into the unknown to chase our passions.

Nope. Please don't do that.

The smarter way? Use your job as a stepping stone, not a stopping point. Take what you already know: your skills, experience, and interests. Find ways to *expand* rather than start from scratch.

If you're a great *writer*, why limit yourself to just writing reports at work? You could freelance, create digital products, or even script videos for brands.

If you're a *social media* queen, you could offer consulting or community management. The key is to identify what's already working for you and monetize it in new ways.

A perfect example? A friend of mine was a fitness coach, helping clients one-on-one. She loved it, but she was *tired* of trading all her time for money. Instead of ditching fitness, she pivoted. She created a digital workout program and started offering online group coaching. Same knowledge, different approach, *way* more income. This is how you start shifting from trading time for money to creating scalable income streams that work for you, even while you sleep. *Who wouldn't want that?*

But let's be real: building a side hustle takes planning, patience, and those extra hours before and after work: a luxury in itself, to say the least. The beauty is, once you get it going, a side hustle can start generating passive income, meaning you're no longer relying *only* on your paycheck. That's the real flex: diversifying your income so you have *options.* Maybe one day, your side gig becomes your main gig. Or maybe it just gives you the peace of mind to know you're not solely dependent on *one* stream of income. Either way, you win.

So, how do you make it happen? First, audit your skills. What do people *already* come to you for? Then, look for ways to package that knowledge differently. Can you create a course, an ebook, or a paid workshop? Can you shift from service-based work to product-based income? Next, use your current paycheck strategically—fund your side hustle, invest in tools, and build a financial cushion. Most importantly, *start*. You don't have to go all in at once; you just need to take the first step. Because at the end of the day, you are not limited to one title, one job, or one way of making money. The more flexible you are with how you use your talents, the more income streams you can build. That, *hermana*, is how you secure the bag *and* keep your peace.

1. Sell What You Already Know

Your day job has likely given you some valuable skills that you might be underestimating. Why not monetize them? If you're on the accounting team, for instance, and Excel is practically second nature to you, consider creating Excel or Google Sheets templates for small businesses, freelancers, or budget-conscious individuals. Spreadsheets with built-in formulas, budgeting templates, or trackers can be incredibly valuable to people who don't have the time or skills to create them from scratch.

Once you create these templates, they're out there working for you. Upload them to platforms like Etsy or Gumroad, set a flat fee, and let them do their magic. With a bit of clever marketing and a dash of carefully researched SEO, these digital products can become a source of passive income with no additional effort on your part.

2. Teach What You Already Know

Maybe you're comfortable on camera or enjoy presenting at work. Amazing. Take those skills and create an online course. Teaching online isn't just for professors; anyone with knowledge in a certain area can make an impact. You could be a project manager, a graphic designer, or even a customer service expert; people are always looking to learn from experienced pros.

Once you record your course, you don't have to show up live every time someone wants to learn from you. Platforms like Teachable, Skillshare, or Kajabi allow you to upload your content, and they handle the payments and hosting. Don't have a social media presence yet? Upload mini-courses on YouTube, build an audience that wants to keep learning from you, and pay you for your knowledge by investing in a masterclass or course. As your course gains popularity, so will your income.

3. Monetize a Hobby

Maybe your passion isn't directly related to your job, and that's okay! Sometimes, the most fulfilling side hustles are the ones that let you escape into a creative space. If you love knitting, painting, woodworking, or any hands-on craft, turn that into a profitable gig. Use your job's steady income to invest in supplies and start small, selling your items on platforms like Etsy, eBay, Facebook Marketplace, or even at local markets around town. It's a great way to indulge your hobby while turning a profit.

By creating a small inventory and posting regularly about your journey, you can get a steady stream of sales while building your personal brand. Once you find a rhythm, this side hustle can bring in consistent, flexible income without becoming another full-time job.

4. Flip Items Online

Got an eye for design or a love for refurbishing? Use your nine-to-five income to invest in second-hand furniture, decor, or electronics that just need a little TLC. With some creativity and elbow grease, you can turn these items into something worth double (or even triple) their original price. Focus on high-quality items that you can easily revamp and set a schedule for your flipping projects so they don't overwhelm your living space or your time.

Once you've built up a small inventory, you can continuously list items for sale. By using platforms like Facebook Marketplace or eBay, you can reach buyers locally or nationwide and earn money from each successful flip. This method requires an initial investment of both time and cash, but it's flexible, allowing you to adjust your commitment based on how much extra income you want to make.

5. Start Freelancing on the Side

Maybe you're a graphic designer, a social media manager, or a writer for your nine-to-five, but you're not totally in love with the projects you're assigned. Why not take those skills and offer them on freelance platforms like Upwork or Fiverr? This allows you to connect with clients who are genuinely excited about the kind of work you love to do. It's also a great way to build a name for yourself and grow a portfolio outside of your main job.

If you find regular clients or projects that align with your skills, freelancing can bring in steady, dependable income. As you get established, you could start to command higher rates or even hire others to help, turning your side gig into a more passive business. The more established you are, the more clients will come to you, so you won't have to spend hours hunting for projects but instead delegating to a team as an agency owner. That has a pretty nice ring to it!

A Few Key Tips to Make It Work

❖ **Start with a Goal in Mind:** Think of this as a stepping stone to more income and independence. Are you looking to pay off debt? Build up savings? Start with a clear financial goal for your side hustle and work backward to figure out what it would take to get there. This will allow you to move with intention and set a clear path.

❖ **Create a Schedule That Honors Both Roles:** Balancing a full-time job with a side hustle takes planning. Dedicate specific blocks of time to your side hustle, so it doesn't feel like it's consuming your entire life. Your goal is to protect the job you currently have, not neglect it. This ensures you're respecting your day job, which is the foundation financing your side venture and keeping a roof over your head.

❖ **Keep It Sustainable:** The goal here isn't to burn out. Your nine-to-five should feel like the launching pad, not the anchor. Find ways to streamline your hustle. Use automation tools, batch-create content, or schedule dedicated "hustle" hours to keep things manageable.

❖ **Visualize the Bigger Picture:** This side hustle is more than just extra cash; it's a bridge to financial freedom. Imagine what you'll do once it's up and running or even sustaining itself without constant attention. Having a clear vision of what's possible will keep you motivated on days when things feel overwhelming.

Camarón que se duerme, se lo lleva la corriente.

If you sit on your skills and wait for the "perfect moment" to start, you risk watching time, and opportunities pass you by. The sooner you start stacking your income streams, the sooner you gain the flexibility and security you've been working for.

Your full-time job isn't just a means to an end. It's the foundation on which you can build something of your own, something that pays off while you sleep, something that lets you create the life you've been dreaming of. Whether it's selling your skills, teaching others, flipping items, or freelancing, your side hustle has the potential to grow, diversify your income, and ultimately give you more choices in how you spend your time and money. Remember, *hermana*, the journey to financial freedom is all about stacking your assets, using your resources wisely, and stepping up one goal at a time.

A Rich Hermana Tip

Listen to your body. Sure, the money is the motive, but if you're burning out trying to do too much all at once, you'll end up using sick days or landing unpaid time off to heal yourself if you get sick. *Trabaja*, but stay on top of your physical and mental needs. It's okay to rest. Rest is what will keep you going.

CHAPTER 17

BREAKING THE SCARCITY MINDSET

"Si te enfocas en lo que no tienes, nunca tendrás suficiente."

For many of us first-gen kids, money has always felt like something you hold onto for dear life. It was never something you use to create opportunities.

We grew up watching our parents stretch every dollar, make meals out of whatever was in the fridge (*arroz con huevo*, anyone?), and work multiple jobs just to make ends meet. That kind of financial stress doesn't just disappear when you start making more money. It follows you. It becomes a mindset.

You get a raise, but instead of feeling relief, you feel anxiety. *What if something bad happens?* You finally have a savings cushion, but spending on anything "extra" makes you guilty, even if it's for something you enjoy. You see someone thriving financially, and instead of being inspired, you feel resentment. *Why them and not me?*

That's scarcity mindset in action. If we don't break out of it, no amount of money will ever feel like *enough*.

Wealth is how you think about money. Here's how we can shift from survival mode to abundance.

Step 1: Recognize Where Your Scarcity Mindset Comes From

Scarcity mindset isn't something we just wake up with. It's learned. For many of us, it comes from growing up in environments where money was unstable, uncertain, or straight-up nonexistent.

Take Luis, for example. His parents always told him to "save every penny" because *you never know what could happen.* Now, as an adult, he makes six figures but still feels guilty spending on things he enjoys, because deep down, he's waiting for everything to fall apart.

Or Carla, who grew up hearing that rich people are selfish and that making money requires *sacrificio.* So even though she wants financial success, she self-sabotages because, deep down, she feels like having more means betraying where she came from.

These beliefs are not your fault, but they are your responsibility to unlearn.

Step 2: Reframe Money as a Tool, Not a Source of Fear

A lot of us treat money like it's *either/or*. Either you spend it, or you lose it. Either you have enough, or you don't. But money is a tool, not a limited resource.

Think about it like this:

Scarcity mindset: "If I spend this money, I'll never get it back."

Abundance mindset: "Money flows. I can make more."

Scarcity mindset: "If someone else is successful, that means there's less for me."

Abundance mindset: "There's enough success to go around."

Scarcity mindset: "I need to grind 24/7 to make a decent living."

Abundance mindset: "I can make money in ways that don't drain me."

The shift happens when you start seeing money as something that moves and grows, not something that disappears the second you use it.

Step 3: Give Yourself Permission to Enjoy Your Money

Spending money just for *fun* can feel…wrong. If you grew up seeing money as something you only use for survival, spending on things like travel, hobbies, or self-care can feel like wasting it.

But the whole point of building financial security is to improve your quality of life.

Instead of thinking, *I shouldn't spend money on this,* try asking:

- ❖ Does this purchase align with my values?
- ❖ Is this something that brings me joy?
- ❖ Am I spending out of fear, or out of intention?

Yes, saving and investing are important. But hoarding money out of fear is still scarcity. It's okay to enjoy the wealth you're building.

Step 4: Drop the "Hard Work = More Money" Lie

One of the biggest lies we were taught is that more effort = more money; that if you're not struggling, you don't deserve wealth.

But here's the truth:

- ❖ Working more hours doesn't always mean making more money.
- ❖ Being busy all the time doesn't mean you're being productive.
- ❖ Resting and enjoying life doesn't mean you're lazy.

The wealthiest people in the world? They're not working three jobs. They're working *smarter*.

Instead of thinking, *I need to work harder to make more money*, shift to *I need to make my money work harder for me*.

That could mean:

- ❖ Investing so your money grows without you constantly working for it.
- ❖ Negotiating your salary instead of just taking whatever you're offered.
- ❖ Creating passive income so you're not trading all your time for money.

Hard work is great, but wealth is built through strategy, not struggle.

Step 5: Surround Yourself with an Abundance-Minded Community

Ditch the friend that's constantly complaining. Scarcity thrives in environments where people constantly say:

"That's too expensive."
"People like us don't make that kind of money."
"Just be grateful you have a job."

If you only hear limiting beliefs, that's what you'll believe.

Start surrounding yourself with people who talk about money differently—people who believe in opportunity, wealth-building, and financial freedom. Whether it's through books, podcasts, mentors, or social media, start filling your mind with:

"There's more than enough money to go around."
"I can make more money in a way that feels good to me."
"I deserve financial security and joy."

Your mindset shapes your reality. The more you feed it abundance, the more you'll start seeing opportunities instead of limitations.

You can learn all the budgeting tips, investment strategies, and side hustle ideas in the world, but if you don't believe you deserve wealth, none of it will stick.

You *deserve* to have money.

You *deserve* to enjoy your money.

You *deserve* to build wealth without burnout.

You deserve to spend time the way you always dreamed of. *Si te enfocas en lo que no tienes, nunca tendrás suficiente.* Focus on what's possible instead.

CONCLUSION

A LETTER FROM THE RICH HERMANA

"Quien se levanta hoy, triunfa mañana."

Hermana, hermano, familia,

If you made it here, *to the very end of this book,* I hope you know how proud I am of you. I wrote this for you. For all of us who grew up translating documents at the kitchen table. For those of us who had to learn about credit, debt, investing, and taxes the hard way. For anyone who has ever felt behind, overwhelmed, or left out of the financial conversation.

You're not behind. You're finally building *intentionally.*

Throughout these pages, we unpacked what it means to be first-gen: to carry your family with you while carving out your own path. We named the invisible weight. We questioned the old beliefs. And we mapped out a new way forward: one that honors your past and supports your future.

You've learned how to create a budget that reflects your life, not just your bills. How to build an emergency fund that protects your peace. How credit works, how investing can start small, and how even taxes (yes, taxes) don't have to feel like a mystery.

But beyond the tools, what I hope you walk away with is a deeper sense of ownership. *Your money story is yours to rewrite.* Your values, your mindset, your vision…these are the real foundations of wealth.

Success isn't measured solely by what's in your bank account. It's how you make decisions. How you reclaim your time. How you empower yourself to say yes to the life you actually want. And if you still feel unsure where to start, that's okay too. Reread the chapters that spoke to you. Revisit the exercises. Take it one step at a time.

Progress is still progress, even when it's quiet. The last pages of this book aren't the finish line. They are the launchpad.

Keep learning. Keep asking questions. Keep giving yourself *grace.* And don't keep this to yourself.

The more we talk about money openly, the more power we give ourselves and each other. Share what you've learned with your siblings, your cousins, and your friends who are just now trying to figure it out. Be The Rich Hermana in someone else's life, too.

I'll continue creating new resources through The Rich Hermana platform so you'll always have somewhere to turn. And if you ever feel stuck, come back to this book. Let it remind you of how far you've come and how much further you can go.

Before you go, I'd love to stay connected.

Follow me on socials @therichhermana and @ixamarpalumbo. Please don't be shy to message me. If you ever need an extra push, a second opinion, or just someone to listen, I'm here. I might not have all the answers, but I'll always try to guide you in the right direction. And if I can't help, I just might know the person who can.

Quien se levanta hoy, triunfa mañana. You're already in motion, and that matters more than perfection.

Here's what I hope you never forget:

You're allowed to be *the first.*

You're allowed to build *differently.*

You're allowed to know more than the generation before you and to *teach* them with *love.*

Most of all, you're allowed to thrive *without* guilt.

You are The Rich Hermana now.

Go build something that lasts.

Con todo mi corazón,
Ixamar Palumbo
The Rich Hermana

ACKNOWLEDGMENTS

To my *mami*, the inspiration behind *The Rich Hermana*. You were my first example of strength, sacrifice, and selflessness. Watching you navigate a new country, work long hours, and still make our tiny house feel like home taught me more about wealth than any finance book ever could. You taught me how to stretch a dollar, how to stretch a dream, and how to lead with *corazón*. This book is as much yours as it is mine.

To my sister, the balancing Libra in our home, the quiet genius behind so many of my "aha" moments. You've always been the steady voice of reason, the one who brought calm to the chaos and asked the right questions when no one else thought to. Your ability to think critically, love deeply, and offer advice that hits *every single time* made you my safe place growing up, and still does. Thank you for reminding me who I am and for always helping me see the bigger picture.

To Peter and Mila, my heart in human form. You two are the love and safety I dreamed of as a little girl.

Peter, you showed me what partnership truly means, not just in the big gestures, but in the quiet, steady ways you show up: holding me when I'm overwhelmed, staying up during my late-night writing sprints, and reminding me who I am when I forget. You never questioned my dreams, even when they shifted, paused, or felt too heavy to carry alone. You just made space, every single time, and pivoted your life alongside mine.

Mila, *mi amor*. This little piece of generational wealth is yours. I'm building it for you. You may be too little to read these pages now, but I hope one day you do. I hope you see how your laughter lit up the hard days and how your tiny footsteps kept me grounded when my mind was racing. You are the reason I fight for a softer, freer future.

To every first-gen *hermana* who sent me a DM saying, "I thought I was the only one": you are the reason I kept writing. Your stories, your courage, and your desire to unlearn and rebuild reminded me that this work is bigger than me. This is for us: for every woman trying to break cycles and build something softer.

To Jenny: thank you for being the kind of talent manager and friend every creator dreams of. You helped me protect my peace and build with intention, and reminded me that I could focus on creating without having to carry it all. Your belief in my voice made this journey lighter, intentional, and a whole lot more fun.

To my team at Mango Publishing: thank you for helping me shape my voice without silencing the parts of me that didn't fit into traditional finance narratives. I've never felt freer in my creative process.

And finally, to my younger self: you didn't have the answers, but you kept going anyway. Look at what we built.

ABOUT THE AUTHOR

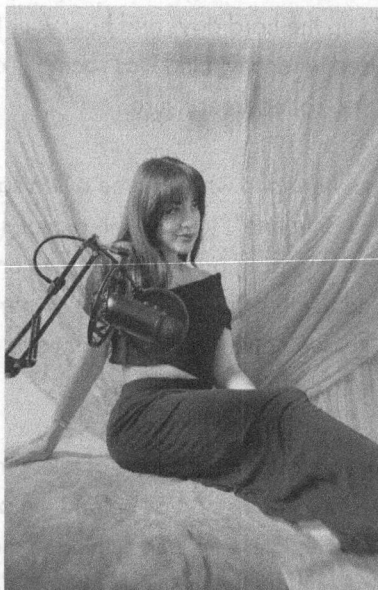

Ixamar Palumbo is a personal finance advocate, marketing strategist, and the force behind The Rich Hermana—a community-first platform helping first-gen daughters of immigrants rewrite their money stories, build financial confidence, and create lives filled with freedom, not just hustle.

Raised by her Venezuelan mother in Miami, Ixamar grew up translating bills, navigating cultural expectations, and learning the US financial system without a roadmap. Her journey from food blogging to financial education began with one simple mission: to make sure other women didn't feel as alone or overwhelmed as she once did.

She holds a master's degree in marketing from Florida International University and a certification in behavioral finance from Duke University, blending strategic expertise with a deep understanding of the emotional side of money. Ixamar breaks down complex topics like budgeting, credit, saving, and investing in a way that feels culturally relevant and emotionally grounded. Her work centers on healing financial trauma, celebrating progress over perfection, and building wealth that feels good…not just looks good. Known as the "big sister" everyone texts at midnight with money questions, she's on a mission to swap shame for confidence and scarcity for possibility.

When she's not scripting her next *"Hay comida en la casa"* video for her social media followers or sending voice-note pep talks about budgeting and belief, she's doing what she's always done best: telling stories that make us feel seen. She got her start behind the camera as a wedding photographer, but like many first-gen daughters with big dreams and even bigger pressure, she realized life had more chapters waiting to be written.

This book is for the *hermana* who's outgrown the box she was put in. It's a love letter to starting over, pivoting with purpose, and choosing yourself again and again. Because building wealth isn't just about money. It's about identity, creativity, and the courage to keep becoming.

mango
PUBLISHING

Mango Publishing, established in 2014, publishes an eclectic list of books by diverse authors—both new and established voices—on topics ranging from business, personal growth, women's empowerment, LGBTQ studies, health, and spirituality to history, popular culture, time management, decluttering, lifestyle, mental wellness, aging, and sustainable living. We were named 2019 and 2020's #1 fastest growing independent publisher by Publishers Weekly. Our success is driven by our main goal, which is to publish high-quality books that will entertain readers as well as make a positive difference in their lives.

Our readers are our most important resource; we value your input, suggestions, and ideas. We'd love to hear from you— after all, we are publishing books for you!

Please stay in touch with us and follow us at:

Facebook: Mango Publishing
Twitter: @MangoPublishing
Instagram: @MangoPublishing
LinkedIn: Mango Publishing
Pinterest: Mango Publishing
Newsletter: mangopublishinggroup.com/newsletter

Join us on Mango's journey to reinvent publishing, one book at a time.